Samuel Francis Smith

My Country 'Tis of Thee

by

Marguerite E. Fitch

illustrated by **Edward Ostendorf**

MOTT MEDIA

Dedicated
to
all Smiths who have
helped make America a great
nation.

Kurt Dietsch, Cover Artist

LIBRARY OF CONGRESS CATALOGING IN PUBLICATION DATA

Fitch, Marguerite E., 1908—
    Samuel Francis Smith: My Country 'Tis of Thee

    (The Sowers Series)
    Bibliography: p. 149
    Includes index.

    Summary: Traces the life of the Baptist clergyman and poet who wrote the words to the patriotic song; "My Country 'Tis of Thee."
    1. Smith, Samuel Francis, 1808-1895—Biography—Juvenile literature. 2. Poets, American—19th century—Biography—Juvenile literature. 3. Baptists—United States—Clergy—Biography—Juvenile literature. I. Ostendorf, Edward, ill. II. Title. III. Series: Sowers.

PS2873.F58 1987   811'.54 [B] [92]   87-42682
ISBN 0-88062-049-8

PREFACE

For many years, I lived in Newton Centre, Massachusetts, where Samuel Francis Smith, author of *America*, had lived one hundred years before me. When the Smith Homestead was threatened to be sold at auction, Newton Public School students brought contributions to my office to help save the Homestead. Our school library contained books about many famous Americans, but none about Samuel Smith. I decided to write a book about him.

The Homestead Society gave me permission to research and copy materials in the Homestead. I photocopied and handcopied documents, articles, and comments by people who knew Mr. Smith. The First Baptist Church granted me permission to research church records of the years when Mr. Smith had been both its minister and church clerk. His language was the flowery variety of his time. Officials at both the Homestead and the church told me that no one else had asked to research materials about Mr. Smith.

Among other interesting details, I uncovered the fact that most historical sources have an error in the date of writing *America*, giving it as 1832. As I tell in this book, the words were written in February 1831, and the song was first performed on July 4, 1831. The error, once made, was compounded as such errors in history often are. Smith himself, in later life, was not always accurate concerning this date.

Also, it is not entirely clear that Christ Church is actually the site of the lantern signal the night of Paul Revere's ride. There is some validity to the claim of another church, called "Old North," which British soldiers destroyed timber by timber.

In 1969 the Homestead was destroyed by fire, and some of the documents I copied from were burned.

Some materials were rescued and taken to the Newton Public Library and the Andover-Newton Theological School.

After I moved to California I had time to begin writing. I also volunteered my services to public schools in the Long Beach Unified School District and other systems. I tell children about Samuel Francis Smith. Most of them do not know about him, although they often sing his words. Both students and teachers have asked where they might find a book about him. I hope this book will now fill their need.

I make grateful acknowledgment to the many people who helped as I researched. It is not possible to name them all, but high on the list must be members of the Marshall family, descendents of Samuel Smith: Mrs. Robert Marshall; John, Edward, and Daniel Marshall; and Miss Jane Marshall. Special thanks are also due to various individuals of the Samuel Francis Smith Homestead Society, Andover-Newton Theological School Library, Newton Public Library, the Jackson Homestead, and these churches: Christ Church in Boston, The Old North Church of Paul Revere Fame; The Second Church in Boston; Andover Baptist Church; Park Street Church; and First Baptist Church in Newton Centre. For other research materials, I am indebted to Miss Madeline Bradley, Mr. Landis A. Nazzaro, and Mr. John W. Stokes.

Editor-writer, Kathleen M. Zaffore, helped me give shape to this story. And my daughter, Mrs. Carolyn E. Jackson, helped with photographing and photocopying my research materials. She and many others encouraged me throughout this project and expressed interest in seeing its completion. Now here it is—for them and for all lovers of *America*.

Marguerite E. Fitch

CONTENTS

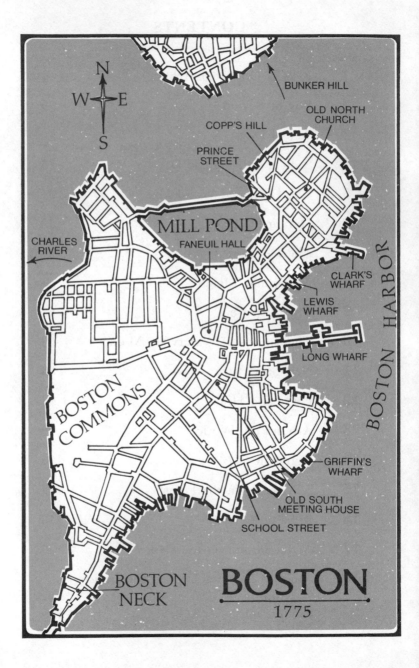

N
W E
S

BUNKER HILL

OLD NORTH
CHURCH

COPP'S HILL

PRINCE
STREET

MILL POND

FANEUIL HALL

CHARLES
RIVER

CLARK'S
WHARF

LEWIS
WHARF

LONG WHARF

BOSTON
COMMONS

GRIFFIN'S
WHARF

OLD SOUTH
MEETING HOUSE

SCHOOL STREET

BOSTON HARBOR

BOSTON
NECK

BOSTON
1775

Bells of Christ Church

DING-dong! DING-dong! ding-DONG! ding-DONNNGGG . . . chimed the eight bells of Christ Church, sometimes called the "Old North Church."

Bright sunlight warmed the chilly April morning in Boston, Massachusetts. The air was clear, and smelled faintly of salt from the nearby harbor. Patches of dirty brown snow melted slowly in the sunshine, sending sparkling trickles of water down the muddy streets. Slippery ice still packed the crevices between the cobblestones. Feathery green buds on the tops of tall elm trees proved that the spring of 1815 was about to arrive in New England.

During the week the streets of Boston bustled with the activities of merchants and sea captains, fishermen and artisans, but today was Sunday, and business had come to a halt. Bells clanged from church towers all over Boston, calling worshipers to services.

Men, women, and children, dressed in their best

hurried along the crooked, narrow streets as worship time drew near. Mr. and Mrs. Samuel Smith picked their way carefully across the icy cobblestone street near Christ Church. "Hurry up, Samuel!" Mr. Smith called to his seven-year-old son who lagged behind. "And watch out for those puddles!"

Samuel had to jog to keep up with the rhythmic clicking of his father's boots on the cobblestones. He giggled as he watched the tails of his father's frock coat flop up and down with each long stride.

Mrs. Smith also found it difficult to keep pace with her husband. With one gloved hand she clutched her gray woolen shawl. The other hand held her black skirts to keep them from dragging on the wet street. Her swishing petticoats rippled slightly whenever she raised them to avoid the mud. A faint scent of lavender trailed after her.

As Samuel hurried to keep up with his parents, he slipped and skidded over the icy patches in his good Sunday boots. He was happy when the steeple on Christ Church came into view. Soon he could rest his legs.

Christ Church steeple was the tallest landmark in the north end of Boston. For many years, sea captains had steered their ships into Boston Harbor by sighting the steeple. As Samuel looked up at the steeple, the golden weathervane gleamed in the sunlight.

"Look, Father!" Samuel shouted, tugging at his father's sleeve. "The weathervane is pointing west."

"Ah, so it is," Mr. Smith replied, "and that means fair weather for today, at least." Samuel and his father smiled at each other in anticipation.

"If we don't go inside soon, we won't find an empty pew," Mr. Smith said, urging his wife and son up the church steps.

"Wait a moment." Mrs. Smith held Samuel at an arm's length in front of her. She inspected the cuffs of his white ruffled shirt. Then she pulled a linen handkerchief from the waistband of her skirt and wiped Samuel's brown buckled boots. "Now you look suitable to go into the church," she whispered to her son and gave him a hug.

"Good morning, friends!" Reverend Eaton's voice boomed above the noisy bells as he greeted the Smith family.

"It is a good morning, indeed," Mr. Smith agreed cheerfully, while extending his right hand to the rector. Timing his words between the ringing of the bells, Mr. Smith added, "And a wonderful day to celebrate God's providence to our country!"

The rector nodded solemnly. "Good morning, Mrs. Smith," he said, smiling faintly, "and—"

"Samuel," Mrs. Smith prompted, giving her son a slight shove toward the rector. Samuel's polite bow was acknowledged by Reverend Eaton's approving smile.

Mr. Smith led the way into the sanctuary, to the boxed pew where the family usually sat. Mrs. Smith entered the pew first. Her skirts rustled as she arranged them around her on the wooden bench. Samuel slid down beside his mother and watched his father quietly latch the door of the high pew. "The old church could be drafty, even on this lovely spring day," Mr. Smith whispered to his son.

As people filed into the pews around him, Samuel recognized neighbors and playmates. He also saw many unfamiliar faces. Christ Church welcomed all worshipers, regardless of denomination. The Smiths were Baptists, but often worshiped at Christ Church because it was near their home.

Soft organ music drifted down from the balcony at

the rear of the church. Pipe organs were rare in Boston, because music was still not allowed in some churches. The Puritans, who were Boston's original settlers, had frowned on the use of music in church. But Christ Church attenders thought music was a dignified part of the worship service. Samuel craned his neck to catch a glimpse of the organ master high in the loft. His father gave him a gentle poke, and with a sigh Samuel turned back.

The organ music faded as the hands of the old Avery-Bennett clock on the balcony pointed exactly to ten. The hush that settled over the church was broken by the soft creaking of the stairs as Reverend Eaton climbed up to the huge wine-glass shaped pulpit.

"Worship will begin today," he announced, "as we sing Psalm 106, 'Praise Ye the Lord.' "

Samuel tingled as the organ music burst joyfully over the congregation. Even the building vibrated with the melodious blast. Samuel liked the music better than any other part of the worship service.

Too soon for Samuel the music ceased, and Reverend Eaton began his sermon. The boy snuggled sleepily against his father, trying to get comfortable on the narrow wooden bench.

"Forty years ago, two lanterns flashed a message from Christ Church belfry that changed history," the rector said. "We are here today because, with God's grace, brave patriots risked and gave their lives for our freedom."

Samuel had heard the story often, and as the rector's voice droned on, he pictured himself on the dark street outside of Christ Church on that chilly April evening in 1775.

Candlelight gleamed from windows at the house across from Christ Church, where young Robert

Newman, the church sexton, lived with his family.
Samuel knew that British officers were billeted at the
Newman home. Loud laughter coming from the
parlor revealed that the soldiers were still awake,
enjoying their pipes and card games.

In Samuel's picture, shoes scuffled softly on the
cobblestones, a figure crept by buildings, hugging
them closely, and someone let out a low, soft whistle.
"Here I am," Robert Newman responded quietly,
stepping out from shadows by the church door. He
motioned his friend to join him on the steps. "I am
ready. What is the signal—one lantern or two?"

"Two lanterns."

Without another word, Robert ducked into the
church. His friend locked the door for his protection
and vanished into the shadows on the street. He
glanced over his shoulder in time to see two lantern
lights flicker high up in the belfry of Christ Church.
A moment later the belfry was dark again, but the
signal had been seen. The patriots had been warned.
The British were coming!

Samuel quivered with excitement as he thought of
the two small brave lights in the church belfry. But
wait! The sound of marching troops broke the silent
night. Robert Newman hid the lanterns and escaped
through a small window. He couldn't chance being
seen leaving through the church door. He dashed
across the street, and climbed over fences and rooftops
until he safely slid through his own bedroom window.
No one at his house had even missed him.

Young William Dawes, a shoemaker, was already
starting his long ride on horseback to warn the countryside. He needed to get safely past British sentries
hidden along the road. In Boston, the streets were alive
with marching troops. Samuel imagined the bold Paul
Revere sneaking through the streets. He was carrying

spurs and wearing heavy riding boots and a short, warm coat. Two men, Joshua Bentley, a boatbuilder, and Thomas Richardson suddenly appeared from a shadowy doorway. The three men quietly made their way to a special hiding place. "Help me here," Paul whispered to the other men. "Pull the bow while I clear some of this brush away." They tugged until the secret rowboat rested in the water. "Hand me the oars," Thomas said. "I'll wrap them with cloth so that no one will hear us rowing." "We must hurry," Paul urged. "The moon is rising and we don't want to be seen by the *Somerset*." The *Somerset*, a mighty British warship with sixty-four cannons, guarded the channel that Paul Revere needed to cross. Two men stepped into the small rowboat, while the third gave a push to launch them. The little boat slid silently into the Charles River, and the third man jumped aboard.

Samuel pretended that he crouched in the brush, watching the little rowboat disappear beyond the *Somerset*. Not a sound broke the silence—not a whistle, or a shout, or a gunshot. The rowboat passed safely and secretly to the opposite shore. Samuel knew that Deacon Larkin's horse waited for Paul Revere, and that soon the patriot would be racing down the moonlit, country road, headed for Lexington and Concord.

"And we can remember that April night proudly and gratefully," Reverend Eaton was saying as Samuel was pulled from Paul Revere back to Christ Church, "and thank God that He has given us freedom to worship Him as we wish, here in America!"

The organ music soared again after the closing prayer ended. Samuel's legs felt prickly as he stood and waited for his father to open the pew door. Slowly the congregation moved down the narrow aisles. Samuel searched the passing faces, and peered up and down each aisle.

"Stay with us, son," Mr. Smith whispered, as the family eased toward the door. Samuel took his father's hand, but continued to turn and lag behind. As the Smiths emerged into the sunlight, Mr. Smith asked, "Are you looking for someone, Samuel?"

"Yes," he replied, tugging his father's frock coat-tails. "Do you see Mr. Paul Revere here today?" he asked, hopefully.

"I'm afraid I don't," Mr. Smith whispered. "He is quite old, and I don't think he comes to church much anymore. But I do see Mr. Joseph Revere, his son. Shall we say hello to him?"

Samuel nodded enthusiastically. He waited patiently while his parents moved around, chatting and greeting their neighbors. It seemed like forever to Samuel before his parents spoke to Paul Revere's son, Joseph.

"Extend my good wishes to your father," Mr. Smith said, as he shook Joseph Revere's hand. Samuel peered out from behind his father's frock coat, but didn't dare say a word about the adventure he had "shared" with Paul Revere during the church service. "I'm sorry he wasn't able to be here on this anniversary of his famous ride."

DING-dong! ding-DONG! DING-dong! DING-donnnggg . . . Sunday worship at Christ Church was over for another week.

Boy of Boston

"May I go to work with you at the barrel shop today, Father?" Samuel asked one morning as the family ate breakfast.

Mr. Smith pursed his lips, and scratched playfully at his curly beard. Samuel grinned at his father's comical expression. "Will you sweep for me today?" he asked the boy.

Samuel nodded vigorously. "And I will carry wood and run errands for you, too."

"Then," said Mr. Smith, slapping the table with his hand, "you may go. If it's all right with your mother."

Samuel turned quickly to his mother. He knew it would do no good to beg. He licked his lips anxiously as he waited for her reply.

"You have some reading to do for Ma'am Richards," she said, "and your school friends will come by to play soon."

"Samuel, you aren't falling behind in your lessons, are you?" Mr. Smith asked, sternly.

"No, sir," Samuel answered. "I like to read and I am good at it. Ma'am Richards likes us to practice at home, though. Mother, I promise that I will do the reading tonight. And I'd rather help Father than play."

Mrs. Smith sighed with resignation. "All right, then."

Samuel leaped up from the table and hurried to get his coat. He enjoyed going to his father's barrel-making shop down on Lewis Wharf. There was always excitement and activity around the wharves to stir his imagination. But most of all he enjoyed spending time with his father.

After Samuel left the room, Mr. Smith saw the worry in his wife's eyes. "Now, Sarah," he said, taking her hand, "if you are concerned that Samuel might get hurt, I can assure you that I'll be careful with him."

"I know, Sam," she said, but the worried expression did not disappear. "You work so hard, and I'm glad that Samuel is willing to help. But he doesn't seem to be interested in anything except helping at the shop and reading. He rarely wants to play with other children."

"You're much too anxious," Mr. Smith said. "Samuel is a bright boy. And a sensible one, too. He is curious and asks many questions. Ma'am Richards says he's the brightest pupil she has."

"But shouldn't he play games with his friends more often?" Mrs. Smith protested.

"Sarah, I think we should encourage him to learn," Mr. Smith said firmly. "I do work hard—long hours of hard labor. Yes, I am well paid for it, but when Samuel is a man, he won't have to labor with his hands. He will be able to use his mind instead." Mr. Smith faced his wife with a determined look as he slipped into his coat. "It's my plan that Samuel will go to Boston Latin School, and then on to Harvard College."

"Harvard!" Mrs. Smith exclaimed.

"I know that we're not wealthy, Sarah," Mr. Smith said, putting his hands firmly on his wife's shoulders, "but my business is remarkably good. I have an excellent partner who brings in his share of contracts, and coopers are always in demand. I'm going to begin saving now for Samuel's college tuition."

"I'm ready to go, Father." Samuel shouted as he ran into the room. Mrs. Smith fastened the cloth coat tightly around her son. Samuel and his father each gave her a hug, and then they were on their way.

The Smith home was on Prince Street, close to Christ Church. Samuel had been born October 21, 1808 on Sheafe Street, only a block away. Even at the age of seven, Samuel could easily find his way around the north end of Boston, and he enjoyed hearing stories about the buildings and landmarks.

Some mornings when he accompanied his father to the barrel shop, they left home early and walked a few extra blocks in order to see some special sight. One of Samuel's favorite walks went past old Faneuil Hall, where the town meetings were held. Patriots met at Faneuil Hall to decide what to do about the tea tax before the Revolutionary War. So many people showed up, though that the crowd was moved to Old South Meeting House instead. There the decision was made to dump the tea into Boston Harbor.

Samuel smiled as he imagined the patriots painted like Indians, spilling tons of tea into the salty water. But what he liked best about Faneuil Hall was the shiny golden weathervane that swung in the wind. It was shaped like a grasshopper.

"Do we have time for a walk this morning,

Father?'' Samuel asked as he trotted behind Mr. Smith. The sun was just above the horizon. Samuel squinted as he and his father headed down Prince Street toward the harbor.

Mr. Smith took the watch from his pocket and shook his head. "Not today, son," he said, tapping the face of the watch. "We are already running late."

Samuel did not argue. He knew that his father valued promptness. Besides, there would be other days for walks.

Prince Street ended at the harbor, and Lewis Wharf was a stone's throw from there. Samuel scampered along with his father, and stopped occasionally to read shop signs and glance into the windows. As they got closer to Lewis Wharf, Samuel's attention was drawn to the great masted ships that lay anchored in Boston Harbor.

"Will ship captains come to buy your barrels today?" he asked, hopefully.

"Perhaps," his father replied.

Samuel ran ahead of his father down the long wharf. Skipping over the wide wooden boards, he reached the warehouse before his father did. It was still early but the door was open and men inside were already at work.

"I can read the sign!" Samuel shouted proudly as his father approached. "It says 'Smith (Samuel) & Urnam (Joseph), Coopers, Lewis Wharf.' "

Mr. Smith tousled Samuel's hair. "That's right, son. Are you ready to go to work? There's the broom."

Wood shavings littered the floor beneath the saw-horses where apprentices carved barrel staves out of oak planks. The staves were placed into forms, and pulled together with rope and a cranking device called a windlass. The windlass creaked and groaned as the

crank was turned, drawing the staves tightly together. A hoop was slipped or pounded over the staves, and the rope was then removed. It was hard work to produce a finely crafted barrel. Around the warehouse, wooden barrels, kegs, and buckets were in various stages of completion.

The shop bustled with activity and noise. Business was good. Barrels and kegs were common and versatile, and always in demand. They were used for storage of every·hing from food to nails, for salting meat, pickling vegetables, churning butter, and for shipping goods around the town or around the world.

Samuel worked his way around the saw-horses and tools as he swept the wood curls into piles. He carefully saved the shavings in a barrel because they could be burned in the fireplace. Keeping the floor clean and the wood piles straight was a never-ending task.

"You can take a little rest break, Samuel," his

father finally told him. Gratefully, he set the broom against the wall and walked out onto the sunny wharf. A great ship docked at nearby Clark's Wharf was being unloaded. Samuel watched muscular men carry off barrels filled with goods from Europe and beyond.

Samuel gazed up and down the waterfront. He knew every wharf along the harbor. Griffin's Wharf was where the tea had been dumped. John Hancock had docked his ships at Clark's Wharf, right next to his father's barrel shop. Spices from faraway lands were unloaded at India Wharf, and the old ship *Old Ironsides* had been built at and launched from Constitution Wharf.

Samuel's thoughts drifted far away, imagining the crack of wind in the sails of a great ship riding the ocean waves. He jumped when he felt the grip of a hand on his shoulder.

"Mother!" he breathed, feeling his heart race. "You scared me!"

"I'm sorry," Mrs. Smith said as she helped the boy to his feet. "It looks like you've been working hard this morning." She pointed to his dusty hands, and then wiped his grimy face with her handkerchief. "Are you hungry?"

"Yes! Is it time for dinner already?" he asked. "I must have been resting out here for a long time. I hope Father won't be angry."

"Of course I won't be, son," Mr. Smith said as he came out of the warehouse behind Samuel and his mother. "You swept and straightened the shop for a long time this morning. You are a good helper."

"But when I took my break," Samuel admitted, looking down at his buckled shoes, "I forgot to come back to work because I was thinking about the ships."

"Sometimes thinking is as important as working," Mr. Smith said, and hugged his son.

"And sometimes playing is as important as working," Mrs. Smith added sternly, looking at her husband. Then she put her arm around her son's shoulders. "Samuel, your school friends stopped by this morning to see if you wanted to go exploring with them to find Mr. Paul Revere's old boat hideout. They said they would look for you again this afternoon."

To Mrs. Smith's relief, Samuel's eyes brightened. "I'd like to go exploring."

"Then you shall," Mr. Smith said. "You may go home with your mother. But do your lessons before you go off with your school friends. All right?"

"Yes, sir!" Samuel said. He hugged his father. While his father and mother talked to each other, Samuel listened to the slapping of little waves against the wharf. Daydreams of ships and the deeds of patriots filled his mind again, and he was already started on his afternoon's adventure.

School Days

Samuel raced across Prince Street, and threw open the door to his house. "Mother!" he shouted. "Mother, where are you?"

Mrs. Smith scurried from the kitchen, her full skirts billowing around her. "Samuel, what's wrong?" she asked, wiping her damp hands on her apron. "Are you all right?"

"I'm fine," he said. "I just wanted to tell you about my first day at Eliot School."

Mrs. Smith threw her head back in exasperation. "The way you were shouting I thought you had chopped off a finger, or had been hit by a cart in the street."

"Oh, no," Samuel said, taking his mother's hands. "I'm sorry if I frightened you. But may I tell you about school?"

"Yes, of course," Mrs. Smith said, and tousled her son's hair. "I never knew anyone could be so excited about school." She led Samuel to the kitchen where she was cleaning vegetables for the soup kettle. "Now, sit here on the stool, and tell me about your first day.''

"It isn't at all like Ma'am Richards' school,'' Samuel said, his eyes wide with excitement. "Everyone already knows how to read and do sums. There are dozens of books we're going to read. And grammar to learn. And we will study poems.''

"Slow down, young man!'' Mrs. Smith said with a laugh. "I can't keep up with what you're saying.''

"Will Father be home soon?'' Samuel asked, looking at the kitchen clock. "I can hardly wait to tell him about school. I never knew how much there is to learn.''

"He should be here any minute,'' Mrs. Smith said, "and I'm sure he will be delighted by your enthusiasm.''

"May I run to meet him, Mother?'' Samuel asked eagerly.

His mother took a deep, slow breath, as she looked at Samuel. Then she nodded her head with a smile. "Yes, go. You're too excited to be of any help to me just now.''

Samuel grabbed one of his new schoolbooks and burst out of the house at full gallop. He knew that the closer to the wharf he found his father, the longer they would be able to walk and talk together before reaching home.

As he hurried along the street he remembered how fearful he had been when his father told him that he had learned everything at Ma'am Richard's Dame-school, and he must now go to Eliot School. Father had encouraged him, saying that Samuel was smart, so the studies wouldn't be too hard, just hard enough to be interesting.

Now, with the first day behind him, Samuel was beginning to understand what his father meant.

"Father!'' Samuel called out as he saw Mr. Smith

come around the corner on the next block. "Father, you were right!" He halted breathlessly by his father's side. "School will be hard, but it is fun to learn. Look at my new book!" Samuel gasped, and thrust the worn volume of poems up at his father.

"Should I read it here on the street?" Mr. Smith asked, smiling proudly at his son. "Or would it be better to take it home?"

Samuel grinned. "I think Mother would be upset if we stayed out late just to read."

"You're not only smart, you are wise," Mr. Smith said. "Let's head home, and as we walk, I want to hear all about Eliot School."

Samuel studied hard, and he proved himself to be an able student. During his first term he composed a poem, *Elegy on a Cat*. The poem rhymed perfectly, which his teacher said was a real achievement for such a young student. Samuel's parents could barely contain their pride.

The next three years raced by. Samuel graduated from Eliot School in 1819, at the age of eleven. He received the school's highest honor, a Franklin Medal, for outstanding scholarship. He also won a gold Prize Medal for composing an English poem. He was already better educated than many adults in Boston, but as far as his father was concerned, Samuel was just starting his real education.

"Son?" Mr. Smith said, tapping the door to Samuel's bedroom. "Are you up and getting dressed?"

"Yes, sir," Samuel called. He opened the door, and joined his father in the hall. He was almost as tall as his father, and looked quite grown-up dressed in his best Sunday clothes. "I didn't have any problem waking up, because I never went to sleep last night. I was too excited."

"And a little scared?" Mr. Smith asked.

Samuel, who was nearly twelve, didn't like to admit fearfulness anymore, but knew that there was no point trying to fool his father. "Yes, Father. I am a little scared. I know that Boston Latin School will be much harder that Eliot, and, of course, everything at school will be new to me."

"Not everything," Mr. Smith corrected. "Some of your Eliot school friends will be enrolling at Boston Latin School with you. That will help."

Samuel was nervous and his stomach ached as he and his father walked across town to School Street. He had often seen Boston Latin School's imposing three-story brick building. He knew about the rigorous education at the school. And he had imagined himself entering the building as one of the students. Now, he and his father opened the massive middle door of the building. What was in store for him?

The door closed behind them, and the room appeared dim. As his eyes adjusted, Samuel saw the headmaster seated at a desk, amidst a shuffle of papers.

"Yes?" the headmaster said, arching his bushy eyebrows and peering over the top of his oval, gold-rimmed spectacles.

"Sir, I would like to enroll my son Samuel for the coming term," Mr. Smith said and stepped toward the desk. "He has graduated from Eliot School, and has received some awards." He displayed Samuel's Franklin Medal, and Eliot School graduation certificate.

"Hmmm, I see," the headmaster said, scrutinizing the certificate and medal. "I presume," he continued, gazing directly at Samuel, "that you already know that Boston Latin School is only for boys."

Samuel was startled, and turned to his father with

a grin. "Does he think I'm a girl?" he blurted out.

Whap! The headmaster's fist slammed down on the desk. "Young man, you should know right now that we have authority to give appropriate beatings to impudent students."

"Excuse me, sir," Samuel stammered. "I-I didn't mean to be impudent." His face burned with humiliation.

"Fill out these forms," the headmaster said, ignoring Samuel's apology, and handing him several sheets of paper. Samuel answered the questions, and returned the papers to the headmaster's desk, without another word.

In a monotone, the headmaster explained, "The purpose of Boston Latin School is to prepare young men to enter college. The curriculum will include Latin, Greek or German, English composition and literature, mathematics, and history. Once a month 'declamations' will be held, when each boy in turn stands before the class and gives a speech."

"Yes, sir," Samuel said, as politely as he could.

"School is held six days a week," the headmaster droned on, "from seven to eleven in the morning, and from one until five in the afternoon. In winter we shorten the day by one hour, and begin at eight o'clock. You may expect to graduate in the Class of 1825, providing your grades are good. Are there any questions?"

"No, sir," Samuel croaked, nervously. "I think I'll like it."

As Samuel and his father walked down the steps of Boston Latin School, Mr. Smith gave Samuel a gentle slap on the back, and smiled proudly. "You are now enrolled in America's first public school."

Samuel immediately became involved with his new studies. He dreaded presenting his first declamation, and too soon, it was his turn. Even though his stomach churned nervously he stood in front of his classmates and in a clear voice said:

History of Boston Latin School

For hundreds of years the Bible could be read only by priests who understood Latin, Greek, and Hebrew. One of the reasons the Puritans came to the 'new world' was for freedom to read the Holy Scriptures in their own language, English. At that time only sons of wealthy men went to school. Usually, they were sent to England to be educated.

Puritan church leaders in Massachusetts were very powerful. They controlled town regulations as well as church affairs. Within five years after Boston was founded, in 1630, church leaders began the first public school, Boston Latin School. From 1635 to 1642 it was the only free public school in America. By the act of 1642, the General Court of the Massachusetts Bay Colony required that 'chosen men of the electorate in each town train children, and take account . . . especially of their ability to read and understand the principles of religion and the capital laws of this country.'

From that time, every township in the Colony was ordered by the Court to appoint a 'master' to teach children to read and write. The town paid the cost. Attendance was not required, but encouraged. Poor men could not always afford to let their sons spend time in school. They were needed to help earn the family living.

When Boston Latin School opened, on April 3, 1635, Philemon Pormort was the 'master.' Only a few students reported to the first class. John Hull was one. His family had come from England, in November, 1635. As soon as they arrived, his parents enrolled him. In John Hull's diary, he wrote that, 'After the little keeping at schoole, I was taken to help my father plant corne, which I attended for seven years together.' He did not tell how much time he spent in school during those seven years, but he learned the trade of goldsmithing. In 1652, by order of the General Court, John Hull was placed in charge of minting coins to replace paper money. Later, he became town treasurer. John Hull became a very rich man.

I consider it an honor and a privilege to be a student in Boston Latin School, from which many great men have graduated.

Secrets on Maypole Day

"We've almost got it!" Mr. Smith said to Samuel. "Stand back while I give it one more whack." The mallet slammed against the metal band, which slipped snuggly into place around the barrel. Mr. Smith wiped the sweat away from his eyes and grinned at his son. "We make a good team."

Samuel helped his father lift the heavy barrel from the form. "We've banded all the barrels, Father, and it isn't even noon yet."

Warm spring air drifted across the harbor into the warehouse. Samuel stood in the open door and gazed longingly toward the center of Boston. It was Maypole Day, May 1, 1820, and a merry holiday for all Bostonians. School was closed, and Mr. Smith's workers had been excused from the warehouse over an hour ago.

Mr. Smith joined Samuel in the doorway and put his arm around his son's shoulder. "Fine spring day," he said. "And a good quiet day to catch up on unfinished work."

Samuel sighed loudly, and turned back into the dark warehouse. He thought about the fun his school friends were having at the Maypole Day celebration.

"The festivities over at Boston Common must be warming up by now," Mr. Smith said, as if he were reading Samuel's mind. "I'm sure there will be games and contests. And, of course, the Maypole Dance will be the highlight this afternoon. It's just the sort of day a boy enjoys."

Samuel, his eyes hopeful, spun around and faced his father. "There's a lot of work for me to do here, isn't there? I don't often have time to help you, because of school."

"Your mother would remind me," Mr. Smith said with a smile, "that there is more to life than work. You study hard and do well in school. Today is a holiday, so, go on to the Maypole celebration before I change my mind."

"Thank you, Father!" Samuel shouted as he grabbed his cap and ran out onto the wharf. His feet pounded the wooden planks like a drum as he galloped toward Prince Street.

"What are you doing home so early?" his mother questioned when Samuel burst into his house.

"Father said I could go to the Maypole celebration," Samuel answered, grinning from ear to ear. "I came home to change into some clean clothes."

"Some of your friends were here a little while ago," Mrs. Smith said. "I told them that your Father might give you the afternoon off. They said that they would wait for you by Christ Church's steps."

"I'd better hurry, then," Samuel said, racing to his room. As quick as a flash, he was changed and ready to leave. His mother handed him some cold meat and bread to eat on the way.

"Be home for supper," Mrs. Smith called after Samuel. He waved his cap and disappeared around the corner.

"I hope they waited for me," Samuel thought as he approached Christ Church. But, to his disappointment, no one was around except Sexton Perry, who was sweeping the steps of the church.

"Mr. Perry!" Samuel called, breathlessly. "Was there a group of boys here earlier?"

"Yes, Samuel," Mr. Perry said, walking up to the boy. "They left about ten minutes ago. They asked me to tell you that they would look for you at the Common."

"Oh," Samuel said, and kicked dejectedly at the dust on the step.

"I'm sure you'll find them," Mr. Perry said. "Why don't you catch your breath for a minute before you run on? Here, sit on the steps. I could use a rest myself," he said, and sat down beside Samuel.

"Aren't you going to the Maypole celebration, Mr. Perry?" Samuel asked.

"I don't think so," Mr. Perry said, with a playful scowl. "I must have some Puritan blood in me. You know, the old Boston Puritans put a stop to the Maypole dance. They couldn't tolerate so much singing and merrymaking."

"But there's been a Maypole Day for as long as I can remember," Samuel said, puzzled.

"And longer than that," Mr. Perry replied. "People started ignoring the old Puritan ban on Maypole Day back before the Revolution was fought."

"I'll bet the patriots had as much fun at Maypole Day as we do," Samuel said, cupping his hand over his eyes and looking up at Christ Church's tall steeple. "Mr. Perry," he asked, as he gazed up toward the belfry, "did you know Paul Revere?"

The sexton shook his head. "Not very well. I rarely spoke to him personally."

"I remember seeing him at church once in a while when I was little," Samuel said. "I always wanted to ask him about his adventures the night he rode to Lexington. Do you know how many riders there were that night?"

"No," Mr. Perry said, shrugging his shoulders, "but I've heard there were several. The more riders there were, the greater was the chance of getting the message to Lexington safely."

"I've always wished that I could've seen the signal lights in the church tower," Samuel confided.

"Come with me," Mr. Perry said, with a hint of mystery in his voice, "—that is, if you aren't in too great a hurry to catch up with your friends." He produced a large, rusty key from his waistcoat, and dangled it enticingly in Samuel's face.

Samuel, eager to solve the sexton's mystery, followed Mr. Perry to the door of the belfry tower. The key turned with a clink, and the door swung open on old, creaking hinges. A narrow steep stairway soared up to the dizzying heights of the belfry.

Mr. Perry started up the stairs, with Samuel at his heels. Slowly, they climbed up and up, passing the eight bells. The stairway was now no more than a shaky old ladder.

"OOOO-oo!" called a low, moaning voice from the dark rafters over Mr. Perry's head. Samuel's spine tingled and he tried to muster the courage to look up. Without warning, something dropped from above.

"Look out!" shouted Mr. Perry. Samuel clung to the ladder and shut his eyes tightly. Something soft brushed his face, and then was gone. "You can open your eyes and come on up," Mr. Perry called to Samuel. "It was just a barn owl."

Samuel's heart pounded in his ears and his legs felt
like jelly. Slowly, he tilted his head back just far
enough to see Mr. Perry kneeling above him on the
belfry floor. "Only a few more rungs," he told
himself, and crept up to the belfry. Mr. Perry held
out his hand to Samuel and helped him through the
trap door into the belfry.

Samuel licked his dry lips, and slowly stood up on
the creaking platform at the top of the tower. Cobwebs
and dust hung heavily in the small, dimly lit room.
As his eyes adjusted to the light, Samuel focused in
the direction Mr. Perry was pointing. There, in a
dusty corner, lay two forgotten lanterns. They were
old and dirty, and the glass of one was broken.

"Oh!" Samuel whispered breathlessly. "Unless I'm
dreaming I must be looking at the signal lanterns."

Mr. Perry grinned, pleased with Samuel's reaction.
He gave Samuel a few minutes to satisfy his curiosity.
"We'd better go down now," he finally said, and
disappeared through the trap door.

The climb down was easier, and soon Samuel and
Mr. Perry were in the vestibule of the church.

Samuel thanked Mr. Perry for sharing the secret
of the belfry. "Do you think Robert Newman would
have let me climb up to see the lanterns?" he asked.

"Probably not," Mr. Perry said.

"Is Mr. Newman buried in Christ Church crypt?"
Samuel asked. He knew that the colonists had carried on an old English custom—burying deceased
church members in the basement beneath the church's
sanctuary.

"No," Mr. Perry told Samuel, "he's in Copp's
Hill burying ground. But Major Pitcairn is buried
here. He's the British officer who led the troops to
Lexington and Concord. Both friend and foe are
honored in Christ Church."

"May I see the crypt?" Samuel asked eagerly.

"You're not afraid to go down there?"

"Of course not!" Samuel replied boldly.

The sexton produced another old key, and led Samuel to a doorway. "Before we go down, we'll need to light a candle." As he entered the dark stairway, Mr. Perry glanced over his shoulder at Samuel. "There won't be any owls down here," he said with a good-natured chuckle.

The crypt was damp and still. Samuel stayed close to Mr. Perry as they moved through the cramped passageways. The sexton's flickering candle cast long, strange shadows that followed them like silent creatures. Samuel shivered.

Mr. Perry stopped and pointed to a tablet on the wall. "Here's Major Pitcairn," he announced, matter-of-factly. "Tomb Number 20."

"Oh," Samuel said softly, swallowing hard. He fought to keep his voice and legs steady, because he didn't dare let the sexton know he was frightened.

Mr. Perry held the candle close to the wall. "When British soldiers were wounded at Bunker Hill, they were brought back across the river to a hospital that was set up on Copp's Hill. Major Pitcairn was wounded, too, and his son carried him to his home on Prince Street. Isn't that your street?" the sexton asked, holding the candle in Samuel's face. Samuel gulped and nodded.

"Anyway," Mr..Perry continued, "Major Pitcairn died of his wounds. Patriots and loyalists alike loved him. Let me show you something else."

Samuel looked over his shoulder nervously. When he turned back, he saw that Mr. Perry had moved away from him in the crypt. With a shudder, Samuel forced himself to walk through the darkness toward the sexton's candle light.

"This is Strangers' Tomb," Mr. Perry said, shining the light up at Tomb Number 41. "It's for people who had no one to claim their bodies. Some were seamen, far from home, or black slaves who had run away from their masters. Some were Indians."

Samuel followed Mr. Perry closely as he groped his way down another aisle. "This is the south wall. There's the Children's Tomb. There weren't many doctors, so children often died."

"I-I should be going," Samuel said weakly. His heart was beating so hard that he was sure Mr. Perry could hear it.

The same ghostly shadows trailed behind them as they returned to the staircase. In spite of the cold air, beads of perspiration clung to Samuel's forehead.

Mr. Perry blew out the candle. The crypt door closed with a thud, and the sexton and Samuel walked together out into the sunshine.

"If you want to see Robert Newman's grave, you'll have to look for it at Copp's Hill," Mr. Perry said. "Or have you had enough exploring for one day?"

Samuel was surprised to see how low the sun was in the western sky. "I don't have time to go to the Maypole celebration now, so I might as well go exploring at the burying ground."

"You've seen the belfry and the crypt," Mr. Perry said, with a twinkle in his eyes. "Here's one more secret to explore: look for Daniel Malcolm's stone. He was a brave patriot who spoke out against British taxes. When the king's soldiers camped on Copp's Hill during the Revolution, they used Captain Malcolm's gravestone for target practice. You can still see the bullet marks."

"Thanks for showing me the lanterns and the crypt," Samuel said. "Now I'll go look for the bullet marks." He hurried toward Copp's Hill so he would have time to look around before the sun set.

The old cemetery dated back to the Puritans. Samuel wove his way through the burial plots, pausing often to read the headstone inscriptions. Some stones were tilted. Others had sunk into the ground so far that names were impossible to read. Samuel found Robert Newman's grave, and then searched for Captain Malcolm's bullet-ridden stone.

The last rays of sunshine cast long shadows across the burying ground. Just when Samuel decided to give up looking for Daniel Malcolm's stone, he unexpectedly happened upon it. Out loud he read the inscription:

A true Son of Liberty
A friend to the Public
An enemy to Oppression
And one of the foremost
In opposing the Revenue Acts of America.

Samuel dropped to his knees beside the stone. Cold, muddy water seeped through his breeches, but he didn't have time to think about what his mother would say when she saw his grimy clothes. After all, they were already dirty from climbing around the belfry and creeping through the moldy old crypt. A little more mud wasn't going to make a difference.

Samuel slid his hands over the surface of Malcolm's stone. His eyebrows shot up as his fingers found the bullet marks. "There they are!" he breathed aloud. "I'll have to come back in the daytime to take a better look at them." He suddenly realized that the sun had set. Darkness in the old burying ground was deepening.

He sprang to his feet and dashed toward Prince Street. "Mother will be worried that I'm not home," he thought. "And when she sees my clothes, I'll probably be in big trouble."

Samuel pushed open the kitchen door gently, and smiled sheepishly at his mother.

"Where have you been?" she demanded, looking at the clock. It was chiming 6:00 P.M. "I've been worried sick."

"I didn't go to the Maypole celebration," Samuel said.

"I know!" Mrs. Smith said, raising her voice. "Your friends came here again late in the afternoon, and told me they hadn't seen you at the Common."

"I went to meet them at Christ Church," Samuel explained, "but they had already left. Sexton Perry and I talked about Paul Revere and the signal lights in the belfry." Samuel decided that it would be best not to mention the perilous climb to the belfry while his mother was upset.

"But you've been gone for hours." Mrs. Smith said with exasperation. "How could you have spent so much time with Mr. Perry?"

"I also went to Copp's Hill to look for Robert Newman's and Daniel Malcolm's gravestones," Samuel said. "Mr. Perry told me how the British used Captain Malcolm's stone for target practice and I wanted to see the bullet marks for myself."

"I think you had better talk to your father when he comes home this evening," Mrs. Smith said with a sigh.

Samuel changed his clothes and washed his face and hands. He returned to the kitchen and ate supper quietly with his mother. Without a word when he had finished his meal, he went up to his room and started studying. But he listened for his father.

It wasn't long before his father came home and Samuel could hear his parents talking softly near the front door. He knew that his mother was reporting the day's events to his father.

A moment later Mr. Smith called, "Samuel, come here now. I want to talk to you."

"Your Mother tells me that you were late coming home tonight, and that your clothes were dirty," Mr. Smith said to his son. "Where were you all afternoon?"

"At the church, talking to Mr. Perry about the Revolution," Samuel said, "and then I went to the burying ground. I forgot all about the time until the sun had set. I apologized to Mother when I got home."

"What did you find so interesting at the burying ground?" Mr. Smith asked, examining his son's face.

"Mr. Perry told me about Captain Malcolm's stone, so I wanted to see it," Samuel explained. "It took me awhile, but it was worth it. His epitaph told how patriotic and brave he was. I memorized it. Would you like to hear it?"

Mr. Smith nodded, and listened intently as Samuel

recited the lines. "Did you see the bullet marks?" he asked, with the familiar twinkle returning to his eyes.

"Yes, but not very well," Samuel replied enthusiastically. "It was too dark. But I'll go back in the daylight sometime to take a better look."

"It sounds as if you learned more from Mr. Perry and your expedition to Copp's Hill than you would have at the Maypole celebration," Mr. Smith concluded, as the mantle clock struck nine. "Time for bed, son. School tomorrow."

Samuel kissed his mother goodnight, and bounded up the stairs. As he said his prayers, he confessed that he hadn't told his parents the whole truth about the activities of the day.

"Maybe tomorrow . . ." he thought, as he drifted off to sleep.

The Darkened Warehouse

Boston sweltered in the late afternoon heat of June, 1823. Samuel slipped out of his waistcoat and mopped the perspiration from his forehead with a handkerchief as he walked slowly down the school stairs.

"Samuel!" a voice called from behind him. "Wait!"

Samuel turned to see a school friend hurrying down the stairs toward him. "What are you doing here so late, Ben?" he asked as the boy caught up with him.

"I was about to ask you the same thing," Ben replied with a laugh. "I stayed to talk with the Greek instructor. I'm afraid I may not pass my exams without some help."

"That's nonsense," Samuel said. "You've been in Greek class with me for three years here at Boston Latin School. You've always done well."

Ben sighed and looked down with embarrassment. "My father has helped me. But now he is ill, and I'm forced to study alone."

"Until he gets well," Samuel said, slapping his friend's back, "I'll be glad to study Greek with you after school. I help another boy, which is why I'm here late this evening. I'm sure he won't mind if you join us."

"That would be wonderful," Ben said, looking relieved. But his face clouded over immediately. "I'm afraid I'll need help for a long time, though, because my father probably won't get well."

Samuel and Ben made plans to meet after school the following day, and then parted company. Samuel started to go home, but suddenly changed direction and walked briskly toward the harbor. Thinking of Ben's sick father made him anxious to see his own father.

Daylight stretched late into the summer evenings, and Samuel knew his father never quit work before dark. He was sure to find Mr. Smith at the warehouse down on Lewis Wharf.

Long before he reached the warehouse doorway, Samuel could hear a mallet pounding bands on a barrel. He stood in the open door and watched his father hammering. The warehouse was stuffy and hot, and his father's shirt clung to his back, drenched with perspiration. Samuel noticed how thin and pale his father looked. He saw his father's chest heave as he tried to catch his breath.

When Mr. Smith looked up, he saw Samuel standing in the doorway. "Son," he called out irritably, "have you come to watch, or work?" Then he quickly tried to cover his impatience by smiling and waving Samuel into the warehouse.

"You look worried, son. What's the problem?"

"I am worried about you, Father," Samuel admitted. "You work so hard, and such long hours. You're always tired. Why don't you come home with me now?"

"I still have a little work to do while it's light," Mr. Smith said, "but I'll come home soon."

"At least stop for a few minutes and get out of this hot, stale air," Samuel pleaded. "It's not much cooler outside, but the air is fresh."

Mr. Smith agreed reluctantly, and followed his son out onto the wharf. "What's this?" Mr. Smith asked, pointing to the stack of books Samuel was carrying, wrapped in his waistcoat. "Haven't you been home from school yet?"

"No, sir," Samuel said. "I stayed late to help a friend with his lesson, and on my way home I decided to come see you."

"Your mother will be worried," Mr. Smith said, "but I'm pleased that you thought of me." He patted his son's back.

"I wish I could help you more often," Samuel replied, looking back into the dark, hot warehouse. "Attending school six days a week doesn't leave much time for work, though."

"You need all your time for study, son," Mr. Smith said seriously. "In fact, your mother is concerned about how hard *you* are working. She sees that your lamp burns late into the night—very often." Mr. Smith reached over and ruffled Samuel's curly hair.

"She must be spying on me through the keyhole," Samuel replied with a laugh.

"I suppose it's natural for your mother to worry about us," Mr. Smith said with a grin, "but I don't want *you* worrying about me, too."

"All right," Samuel said with reluctance, "but only if you'll come home with me now."

"The evening is disappearing quickly," Mr. Smith said, and checked his pocket watch. "I suppose I can close up early one night."

Samuel helped his father straighten up the

workshop. Mr. Smith gathered his account books, and
the two of them headed toward Prince Street.

"You say you're tutoring at school, son?" Mr.
Smith asked as they hurried along Fleet Street.

"Yes, in Greek," Samuel answered. "It's helpful
for my own study as well as for the boys I tutor."

"How many languages are you studying?"

"Three," Samuel said. "Latin, Hebrew, and of
course, Greek."

"I'm glad that you enjoy school," Mr. Smith said
proudly, "and that you are doing well enough to help
other boys. Are you still writing verses?"

"Oh, yes," Samuel said with a laugh. "And not
just about cats."

"Let me do the explaining, Samuel," Mr. Smith
said as he reached for the doorlatch of their home.

"Samuel!" Mrs. Smith shouted as the two walked
through the door.

"Look, Sarah!" Mr. Smith said playfully. "I
brought this tall, gangly youth home with me. He
wanted to help me at the warehouse, but I told him
he looked better suited to be a scarecrow in the kitchen
garden. So I brought him home to you. Just look at
those long arms with the shirt sleeves above his
wrists."

"That's not amusing," Mrs. Smith protested. "I
have been worried about both of you—Samuel so late
from school, and you working yourself to death at the
warehouse."

Mr. Smith hugged his wife and comforted her.
Then they all sat down to supper. It was unusual for
the Smiths to dine together on a weeknight, and they
enjoyed each other's company. As soon as they finished the meal, Mrs. Smith cleared the dishes. Mr.
Smith opened his account books and Samuel retreated
to his room to study, glad that his father was home
early for a change.

For the next several evenings, Samuel went directly from school to the warehouse to help his father. One evening he arrived a little later than usual.

"Sorry I'm late, Father," he apologized as he slipped into his work apron and rolled up his sleeves.

"Is there something wrong, son?" Mr. Smith asked, looking at Samuel's troubled face.

"Nothing I can't make up," Samuel said. "I didn't do well on an exam today."

"That settles it," Mr. Smith said, taking Samuel by the arm and leading him back to his stack of books on the office desk. "I have my job as a cooper and you have yours as a student. You must go home right now and study."

"But, Father—" Samuel argued.

"Don't argue with me. Do as I say," Mr. Smith continued seriously. "Your education is more important to me than your help in the warehouse."

Reluctantly, Samuel removed the apron and gathered his books. "Please don't work too late, Father," Samuel pleaded as he picked up his books and headed out the warehouse doorway. Slowly he walked along Fleet Street, then to North Street, and finally dragged along Prince Street.

He couldn't concentrate as he bent over his books that evening. His mind kept wandering and he listened for the chimes on the mantle clock downstairs. When it struck eight, Mrs. Smith rapped sharply on her son's door.

"Your father is never this late," she said, her face lined with worry. "It's dark, too."

"I'll go back to the warehouse and insist that he come home," Samuel volunteered, sharing her concern.

When he reached the wharf, he could see his father's shop was dark, as if it were closed for the night.

"Maybe I passed him on the way," he thought hopefully. But as he drew closer to the warehouse, he saw the large doors opened wide.

"Father!" he called into the vast darkness. "Are you in there?" His voice echoed emptily among the towers of barrels. "Father!"

There was still no answer. Samuel hesitantly entered the black warehouse. He reached out into the darkness, groping his way toward the little office where he could find a lamp.

He edged around a tall stack of barrels. "Oh!" he gasped breathlessly as he stumbled over something soft. He caught his balance just before he fell. Cautiously he reached down and his fingers touched soft clothing. His father was lying in a heap on the floor.

Samuel dropped to his knees and threw his arms around his father. "What happened?" he cried out as he gently shook his father. When he placed his ear to his father's chest there was no heartbeat. "Don't die!" he screamed.

Samuel's long legs wobbled when he stood up. He swallowed great gulps of air to fight back the terror. His heart beating madly, he ran out onto the wharf and headed for home. He found his mother standing in the doorway, just as he had left her.

"What happened? Where is your father?" Mrs. Smith shrieked as Samuel ran up and threw his arms around her.

"Father is lying on the warehouse floor," Samuel explained. Then crisply he added, "I'm going to get Dr. Boynton. We must get Father home. Ask some neighbors to help."

Within an hour, Mr. Smith was stretched out on the parlor sofa. Dr. Boynton listened to his patient's faint breathing. Deep, concerned lines etched his face.

"Take your mother to the kitchen, Samuel," he said. "Make some tea. I'll stay right here until I know—" his voice trailed off as he looked away from Samuel and Mrs. Smith.

Time dragged. The mantle clock struck twelve. At last Dr. Boynton appeared in the kitchen doorway, looking tired and defeated.

"I'm sorry, dear friends," his voice cracked. "I tried my best, but there was nothing I could do. His heart simply quit."

Mrs. Smith collapsed against Samuel, sobbing helplessly. Tears streaked Samuel's face, too, as he held his mother. "I can't believe it," he whispered over and over. "What will we do without him? What will *I* do without him?"

Dr. Boynton's satchel snapped shut. "I will take care of the necessary arrangements," he told Samuel softly. "Come to me if I can help you with anything."

Samuel nodded. "Thank you, Dr. Boynton, for trying—" he murmured, tears choking his voice.

The front door closed quietly. Samuel led his mother to her rocking chair. He knelt beside her, gently stroking her hand. "No one can take Father's place," he said, "but I will do my best to help you."

Mrs. Smith wiped her eyes, and gazed appreciatively at her son. "I think I will go lie down," she whispered as she rose from her rocking chair. Samuel walked with her to the bedroom. He covered her with an afghan and kissed her forehead. Her quiet sobs added to his feeling of loneliness and dejection. Tears ran down his face as he prepared a list of duties for himself.

When daylight's first rays crept through Samuel's window, he set aside his quill pen. Quietly he went to his mother's bedroom and laid a scrap of paper on the table beside her bed. "It will be the first thing she sees when she wakens,'' he thought. Samuel had written:

> Bereaved, but bowing to our lot,
> Our onward path we tread,
> And mournfully, we gather up
> The mantle of the dead.

Harvard College

The days following Mr. Smith's death were trying for Samuel and his mother. There was so much to be done, and so many different decisions to be made.

"I'm glad that you approve of Mr. Urnam's offer to buy your father's share of their partnership in the barrel shop," Mrs. Smith told Samuel, sighing with relief.

"Father would want us to sell it, I'm sure," Samuel said. "I'm too young to take over his share of the business, and I really have no interest or skill in it."

"Futhermore, your father wanted you to continue your studies," Mrs. Smith said, "and he hoped that you would attend Harvard. The money from the sale of the business will allow us to live until you have a profession. But I'm afraid you'll have to work some to help pay for your tuition."

"That's all right, Mother," Samuel replied. He opened a small book and showed her a list of names. "Since I'm already tutoring several students, I could easily add a few more in order to earn some additional money. And I have been praying for the Lord's help. I know He will care for us.''

Samuel's college education would prepare him to seek a profession, rather than to become a craftsman, like his father. Boys did not always follow their fathers' trades anymore. Having college educations, they could branch out into new fields. Boston had grown to be an important and influential city in the new nation, offering opportunities in many new fields.

Most of Samuel's school friends expected to continue their educations at Harvard College, just across the river, in Cambridge. It seemed natural that Samuel, too, would attend Harvard, not only for himself, but because that had been his father's greatest dream.

Samuel studied hard during his final two years at Boston Latin School. He learned three more foreign languages, and continued tutoring several classmates. By the time he was seventeen, Samuel had achieved a well-earned reputation around Boston as a linguist. He also wrote articles and poems which were occasionally printed in local Boston newspapers.

The enforced ''declamations'' at Boston Latin School trained Samuel to become an excellent public speaker on many subjects. He enjoyed conversing with people, too. He respected other people's opinions, no matter what his own views might be. His warm, friendly manner and quick humor produced friendships which continued throughout his lifetime.

One late summer morning, as the sound of insects hummed along the Charles River, Samuel hurried across the dewy grass toward the imposing buildings of Harvard College. He thought about the last time he had been a new student in a school. His father walked at his side and introduced him to the headmaster at Boston Latin School. Today, in September,

1825, he was walking to a new school alone.

"Father would have liked to be with me today," he thought. "Thank you, Lord," he whispered, "for giving me a father who encouraged me to learn so that I could enter this great school, Harvard College."

Only twenty young men entered Harvard College that fall. Because there were so few, they seemed more like brothers than classmates. Formal first names were shortened. Samuel became "Sam" to them, but never to his mother. The group nicknamed themselves "the boys."

Among Sam's classmates were James Freeman Clarke, Samuel May, Charles Sumner, George Bigelow, Wendell Phillips, Ben Pierce, Ben Curtis, John Motley, and Oliver Wendell Holmes. Although Sam loved all of them, his dearest and closest personal friend was Oliver Holmes. Like Sam, Oliver enjoyed writing and talking. Oliver also wrote verses and was named the class poet.

Before Samuel could hardly realize it, one year at Harvard was nearly behind him. He thought about it as he tucked his books under his arm and walked out into the spring sunshine. He knew he had done well in his studies, but somehow he felt troubled. Walking along the river bank he found a dry, grassy spot, where he dropped his books and settled down beside them to think.

"Oh, there you are!" It was the familiar and welcome voice of Oliver Holmes. "Ben said he saw you headed this way and he thought you looked as if you'd lost your best friend. I decided to find you before you cast yourself into the river." Oliver laughed merrily and sat down on the grass.

Sam shook his head and smiled. "I do have a problem," he confessed, "but it's nothing serious, yet. I have no idea what profession I should choose."

"Neither do I," Oliver rejoined. "I figure that I have at least three more years to worry about it."

"That's true," Sam agreed, "but it seems that I should have at least a general idea, like writing or teaching."

"Face it, Sam," Oliver said with a chuckle, "you are too good at too many things. That's your problem. You can do just about anything you want. But it should include talking, because that's what you do best."

"Maybe," Sam said, his eyes twinkling, "but I have to be able to make a living at it."

"Then become a statesman or a minister," Oliver said. "In fact, you are so good at learning languages, you ought to be a missionary to some tribe on the other side of the world."

"You may laugh at me," Sam said seriously, "but I have thought of doing just that."

Oliver's eyebrows shot up.

"But I've also thought about being a poet," Sam added. "And when I was a boy, I dreamed of being a patriot, risking my life for American freedom."

"Not a bad ambition, even for a Harvard man," Oliver said. The two young men sat quietly beside the river for several minutes before Oliver headed back to his room.

Sam quoted to himself from the many Bible verses he had memorized. He thought for a while upon Proverbs 3:5 and 6—"Trust in the Lord with all thine heart; and lean not unto thine own understanding. In all thy ways acknowledge him, and he shall direct thy paths." Yes, God would help him know which "path" to take. But for the present, he could almost hear his father's words: "Your job is to be a student."

Sam continued to learn more foreign languages—a total of thirteen in all. He gained a wide reputation as a linguist. Dr. Lieber, editor of the first *Encyclopedia Americana*, asked him to translate over a thousand pages for the encyclopedia from a German book titled *Conversations Lexicon*. This was published during his senior year, 1829.

Along with his translation work, Sam continued to write articles for magazines and newspapers. Fellow students who were failing in various subjects constantly asked him to tutor them, which helped him earn his college tuition.

While Sam was attending Harvard, Boston churches were awakening to the joy of good music in the worship of God. Sam, who had always loved the rumbling pipe organ at Christ Church, was delighted to see organs and choirs become accepted in the churches.

The leader of this new interest was a young man named Lowell Mason. Lowell opened several private schools of music, which attracted many students, and his classes became very popular. He organized church singing groups that sang for enjoyment as well as to provide good church music.

Although Lowell Mason was several years older than Sam, they met through students whom Sam knew and who attended Lowell's classes. Sam immediately liked Lowell's charming, quiet manner, and admired his great musical ability. Sam's warm personality, and his ability to translate languages were attractive to Lowell.

During Sam's final year at Harvard, he and Lowell saw each other often, and Sam was the first to learn Lowell's good news.

"I've been offered the position of organist and choir director at the Park Street Church near the Common," Lowell said with pride.

"I'm pleased for you, Lowell," Sam responded

warmly. "Everyone says you are *the* musical leader in Boston."

"I'm not so sure about that," Lowell replied modestly, "but I have several ideas I want to discuss with you, Sam. One is to do something for children— establish a Sabbath School for religious education in Bible and music."

"Great idea!" Sam agreed enthusiastically. "I know you'll be successful. When do you plan to start?"

"I have to go slowly," Lowell continued. "This is a whole new concept, and I'll have to convince the church members that it's worthwhile."

"If I can help you in any way, just let me know," Sam offered eagerly.

"I'll remember that offer, my friend," Lowell responded, slapping Sam on the back.

As Harvard graduation drew near, the Class of '29 was both sad and glad. "The boys" gathered often in each others' rooms to discuss their careers.

"We've been so close for four years, it will be difficult to separate," Sam remarked sadly. "Some of us have been together for ten years—as far back as our first year at Boston Latin School."

Ben Curtis changed the mood. "George Bigelow and I are going to study law," he said confidently. "If you fellows ever get into trouble, come see us. We'll take care of you." The boys laughed loudly.

"I plan to be a teacher," Ben Curtis said. "What about you, James?"

"I'm hoping to go to seminary and enter the ministry," James Clarke replied.

"That's my goal, too," Charles Sumner added.

Jovial Oliver Holmes gave Sam a gentle nudge. "I think you should be a minister, too. I can remember discussing this with you on the river bank several years ago."

"I'm still leaning in that direction, but I haven't decided yet," Sam admitted. "What about you, Oliver?"

"Undecided." Oliver paused dramatically and then laughed. "If I could make a living writing poems, that is the career I would choose. But that's impractical." Oliver smiled at Sam. "I'll wait until Sam makes up his mind before I decide."

On graduation day, 1829, honor after honor was awarded to Samuel Francis Smith. His mother watched with proud and tearful eyes. At supper that night, she said simply, "I wish your father could have seen his dream fulfilled today. He would have been proud of you."

"I'm glad you think so, Mother," Sam said as he squeezed her hand.

"And now that you have all this knowledge stored in your head, what will you do with it?" Mrs. Smith asked.

"This afternoon I was offered a position as writer for a Boston newspaper," Sam said.

"That's wonderful!" Mrs. Smith said, clapping her hands in surprise. "But you don't sound eager about it."

"I'm not certain what I want to do, Mother," Sam confessed. "For now, I'll work on the newspaper, write articles, do some translation and interpreting, and maybe some tutoring. That will support us. But I need time, Mother, to decide what my life's work will be."

"You must do whatever is best for you," his mother replied quietly.

"Yes, I must," Sam agreed.

The Decision

Sam dipped his quill pen and stared out the grimy window of the newspaper office. The clanging of the printing press in the next room interrupted his thoughts. He read again the sentences he had scribbled on the paper before him, but his mind wandered before he began to write again. His thoughts seemed as dreary as the weather.

The door flew open, and a cloaked figure dashed in out of the rain. "Ho! Sam Smith! I've come to rescue you on a rainy afternoon."

"Oliver!" exclaimed Sam, leaping up from his desk to meet his best friend. "I didn't expect to see you until Saturday."

"True, that's when we usually meet," Oliver said. He walked across the office in two long strides and peered at the unfinished article on Sam's desk. "But after our talk last weekend about your work here at the newspaper, I decided that you needed an afternoon off. Get your coat."

Sam didn't need a second invitation. A few minutes

later, he and Oliver were sloshing across the cobbled streets of Boston together. Oliver led the way to a tea shop where an inviting fire roared in the grate.

"Settle yourself here, Sam," Oliver said merrily, "and let the day's cares go up the chimney with the smoke."

"Always the poet," Sam said, and gladly took the seat closest to the fire. The shop's mistress brought a steaming pot of tea and a plate of cakes and set them on the table.

"Now," Sam said, smiling knowingly at his friend, "maybe you'll tell me the real reason for this sudden visit."

"I can't fool you, can I?" Oliver said with a chuckle. "I have some news and it's a little sad. Ah! If only we could make a living writing verses!"

"John Greenleaf Whittier does," Sam said, "but I'm afraid he's the exception rather than the rule."

Oliver nodded. "Rhyming comes easily to you and me, but I'm afraid it won't be my career. My news is that I'm thinking of studying law for a year, but I doubt that law will be my career."

"You'll be good at the law," Sam encouraged, and thrust his right hand toward Oliver. "Congratulations on your decision."

"But what about you?" Oliver asked. "You aren't satisfied working in the newspaper office. Have you given any more thought to your career?"

"Thought and prayer," Sam said.

Sam and Oliver drank tea and talked for over an hour before parting company. Sam waved as Oliver disappeared into the misty afternoon. He pulled his coat collar up around his neck and thought about returning to the newspaper office. Instead, he set off in the opposite direction, walking briskly toward the harbor until his bootheels thumped against the wide planks of Lewis Wharf.

The faded and weatherbeaten sign still swung above the door to his father's warehouse. He rubbed the dirty glass on the double doors and peered into the dark shop. It was empty.

"Father taught me so much," he said softly, "and guided my decisions wisely. I wish he were here now." Sam turned abruptly and pushed his hands deep into his pockets and headed home.

As he passed Copp's Hill, brilliant sunlight spilled through the clouds, and the rain ceased. He wandered toward the rock at Lookout End where he had spent many hours as a teenager. Shading his eyes from the sun's low rays, he sighted the weathervane on Harvard College. Across the river was Charlestown and Bunker Hill. To the east he watched the ships on the grayish green waters of Boston Harbor. To the south were the thickly wooded Blue Hills. Beyond them was Plymouth, land of the Pilgrims.

In the burying ground, damp autumn leaves had formed a spongy mat which coated the walkways between the graves. Sam treaded quietly between the gravestones, reading the epitaphs he knew so well. Thoughts of his father flooded his memory again.

"Father wanted me to know that these brave and noble men sacrificed their lives for freedom—and for me," he thought as he fingered the bullet holes on Captain Malcolm's grave. "I want to serve, too. But how?"

Just then, the clear, soft, silvery sound of the bells of Christ Church filled the air. Sam listened. "God is guiding in my decision," he thought. "Yes, I should become a minister. Perhaps I can teach people to know the Lord and to love our wonderful country too." Sam smiled and, with lighter steps, headed home. He had news to share with his mother.

Sam shook the last raindrops off of his coat and

hung it in the kitchen to dry. He entered the parlor and found his mother rocking by the fireplace.

"I don't need to ask where you've been," Mrs. Smith remarked cheerfully when she saw two red leaves clinging to her son's trousers.

"To the familiar places," Sam said. He smiled as he brushed the leaves into the fire. "I walked down to Father's warehouse. The sign is still there, but quite faded. I'm glad I worked with him. From there I walked through Copp's Hill." He looked into his mother's face and said calmly, "I've come to a decision about my life's work."

She stopped rocking. "Yes?" she inquired as if expecting her son to continue.

Sam knelt and took her hand. "I want to be a minister. I've been thinking about it for a long time, but this afternoon the Old North Church bells brought me to my final decision."

"Does that mean more schooling?"

"Yes, Mother. I'll need training—at least two years. It's too late to enter Andover Seminary this year, but a year from now I'll go."

Mrs. Smith patted Sam's hand. "I hoped you would find a nice young lady and get married."

Sam laughed. "Seminary first," he said, "then romance." He went to his room and after he closed the door, he knelt beside his bed. A feeling of peace flooded over him.

A Familiar Melody

The stagecoach lurched and bumped over the rutted road. Red and gold leaves swirled in the dusty wake of the coach, and then blew away in the brisk September wind.

Sam tugged at his beard and gazed out of the coach at the passing farms and villages. He was the only passenger in the coach as it rumbled toward Andover. He reached into his coat pocket and removed a letter.

Dear Mr. Smith,

We are pleased to inform you that you have been admitted to Andover Seminary as a theology student. Your course of studies will begin in September, 1830, and will be completed in two years.

Sincerely,
The Register
Andover Seminary

Sam folded the letter and replaced it in his pocket. He smiled. Soon he would be a student again.

The stage stopped at small towns along the way to

deliver and take on mail and a few packages. At each stop Sam jumped out and stretched his long, aching legs. Occasionally there was someone to talk to while he waited for the stage to leave again.

At mid-afternoon, the stage jolted to a stop once more.

"Andover, sir," the coachman called to Sam. Sam climbed down, retrieved his satchel and books, and paid the driver. There was no need to inquire the whereabouts of the Seminary. The brick buildings stood right in front of him. Sam stamped the dust from his boots, and climbed the steps to the entrance of the largest building.

The Registrar's office was quiet, and empty, except for one man seated at a desk.

"You must be Samuel Smith," the Registrar said the moment Sam walked through the door. "We've been expecting you. You're the last student to arrive. Sign in here."

Sam took the pen from the Registrar's outstretched hand and signed his name at the bottom of the class list. "I'll need a place to live," Sam said.

"Look on the bulletin board," the Registrar replied, pointing across the room. "You'll find notices from several people who have rooms to rent."

Sam examined the notices carefully. "Excuse me," he called to the Registrar, who had returned to his work. "Do you know Mrs. Hitchings? Would you recommend her?"

"I'd say her quarters are as good as any," the Registrar mumbled without raising his head. "Her house is just a few doors down the street."

"Good," Sam said cheerfully, as he copied several names onto a list. "I'll try her home first. Now, can you tell me about classes, sir?"

The Registrar handed Sam a printed schedule.

"Classes begin tomorrow. Good day, Mr. Smith," the Registrar said, dismissing Sam.

Sam let out a sigh of relief as he dropped his heavy bags on the Hitchings' doorstep. He knocked, and a moment later the door opened. A plump, motherly woman smiled at him as she pushed wisps of straggly hair from her face. "You're here to see the room, I suppose?" she asked. Wiping her forehead with a long, white apron, she stepped aside so that Sam could enter.

"The room is in the front, facing the street," Mrs. Hitchings said as she led the way. "There's good light from morning to sunset."

The room, though bright and clean, had little furniture—a bed, a dresser, and a table with a straight chair in front of the window. A small braided rug beside the bed offered the only covering over the painted floor boards. A rocking chair in the center of the room reminded Sam of home.

"It'll do," he said. "It seems like a good, quiet place to study."

"Many students have thought so," Mrs. Hitchings said defensively, "but I can't let you have it until I know something about you."

"Of course," Sam agreed. "My name is Samuel Francis Smith. My friends call me Sam, and I hope you will, too. My home is in the north end of Boston near Copp's Hill, where my mother still lives. She's a widow."

"You're not married, then?" Mrs. Hitchings asked, her eyebrows arching in surprise.

"No, not yet," Sam replied with equal surprise at the personal nature of her question.

"And such a handsome young man! How have you managed to stay single?"

"I haven't had time for courtship—yet," Sam

explained in embarrassment. He felt his face growing hot clear up to his hairline. "So far, education has been the center of my life."

"That will change," Mrs. Hitchings predicted, holding out her hand for Sam's rent money. Abruptly she changed the subject. "From now on, you'll be a part of this family, Sam. Breakfast is at six o'clock. Dinner is at noon and supper at six in the evening. Be prompt. Mr. Hitchings doesn't like to wait for his meals. Now, bring in your bags and then come to supper."

"I'll do my best to come to meals on time, Mrs. Hitchings," Samuel pledged, bowing slightly.

Sam quickly slipped into the daily routine in the Hitchings' home and at the seminary. He wrote to his mother every day, and to Oliver Holmes once a week. Oliver wrote that he left law school, and had decided to become a physician.

Because Sam had a well-established reputation in the Boston area as a writer, he was continually in demand to write for magazines and journals. The money he received for his articles was his only income.

Fall faded into a dreary, cold winter. The only heat in Sam's room was what seeped in from the fireplace in the parlor across the hall. He often brought a piece of heated soapstone from the back of the kitchen stove to put under his feet while he studied. Before he crawled into bed, Sam would shove the soapstone between the icy sheets.

On a cold day in February, 1831, Sam sat at his study table. His heavy overcoat hung on his shoulders. Sam kept rubbing his fingers to keep them from stiffening. A loud knock at the front door startled him.

Chilly wind raced through the hall as Mrs. Hitchings called, "Sam, you have a visitor."

Sam's chair scraped the wooden floorboards as he

pushed away from his table and rushed to greet the
visitor. "Lowell Mason!" he exclaimed, firmly
grasping his friend's hand. "What brings you all the
way to Andover on such a miserable day? I hope it's
not bad news. Is my mother all right?"

Lowell laughed and slapped Sam on the shoulder.
"Your mother is fine—lonely for your company, of
course. She's looking forward to spring vacation when
you'll be home. I came to Andover to ask you to keep
a promise."

"A promise?" Sam asked, scratching his head
thoughtfully.

"Perhaps you've forgotten," Lowell said. "A cou-
ple of years ago you offered to help me any way you
could with my Sabbath School."

"Of course!" Sam exclaimed. "And I meant it.
What may I do?"

"I need to have some German songs translated,"
Lowell replied eagerly. "You know that I'm not strong
in languages. But, then, I doubt that you could write
music." Lowell and Sam laughed together.

Lowell explained, "I plan to teach some patriotic
songs to my pupils at the Park Street Church. Next
July 4, Independence Day, we'll have a celebration
with a musical program."

"I'll be happy to help," Sam said. "Where did you
get German songbooks?"

"From Mr. William Woodbridge," Lowell replied.
"He visited Germany recently to compare their public
schools with ours. He knows about my Sabbath School
choir, so he brought the songbooks to me." Lowell
handed the books to Sam. "Now, tell me how you
like being in Andover Seminary. Are you still happy
with your choice of being a minister?"

"Yes, and more sure than ever," Sam proclaimed
loudly.

Sam and Lowell talked for a long time about classes and Boston news and mutual friends. The grandfather clock outside Sam's door chimed twelve.

"Mrs. Hitchings serves dinner at twelve," Sam said. "I know she would welcome a guest. Can you stay?"

"Thanks," Lowell said, slipping into his overcoat, "but I'd better wait for the stage. It leaves in half an hour, and I don't want to be stranded here in a bad storm."

"Until vacation, then," Sam agreed, and he accompanied Lowell to the front door.

"Thanks for the favor," Lowell called as he hurried down the steps into a flurry of snowflakes.

Sam gulped down his dinner and anxiously returned to his study table. He pushed aside the notes and papers for the next day's classes and opened the German songbooks. As he turned the pages, he hummed the tunes.

"Here's a familiar one," he said to himself. "M-m-m. I've heard it often at Christ Church. M-m-m—a German patriotic song." He reached for his quill pen and picked a discarded envelope from the wastebasket beside the table. Within half an hour he had composed five verses that matched the tune. He slipped the scrap of paper inside the songbook, then went on to translate the songs Lowell had marked. By the time he finished, the snowy afternoon had faded into dusk. Glancing at the hall clock, Samuel exclaimed, "Suppertime already?" He walked to the dining room, still humming tunes.

The Surprise

On his way to the Fourth of July celebration in 1831, Samuel walked past many familiar places. He saw the grasshopper vane pointed steadily west. Strolling up School Street, he passed Boston Latin School. At the corner of Tremont Street he gazed at the huge marble columns of *King's Chapel*, where English monarchs had worshiped before the Revolutionary War.

As he approached Park Street Church, he saw hundreds of people already gathered in front of the church and on Boston Common. Horse carriages lined both sides of Tremont and Park Streets. The flag on the State House snapped smartly in the soft breeze of the warm summer day. By the time Samuel found a place where he could see the front of the church, it was time for the exercises to begin. He looked around at the huge crowd and knew that Lowell would be pleased.

Although printed copies of the program had been circulated among the crowd, there weren't enough for everyone. Sam did not mind that he didn't get one, because he already knew the songs that would be sung.

Excited children bobbed up and down on the church steps, taking their places in the choir. Lowell was standing on a box, facing the children. When he gave the signal, two hundred children rose to their feet. Their clear young voices rang out:

> My Country, 'Tis of Thee,
> Sweet land of Liberty,
>   Of Thee I sing:
> Land where my fathers died,
> Land of the Pilgrims' pride,
> From every mountain-side,
>   Let freedom ring.

"My verses!" Sam gasped. "I must have left them in Lowell's book." Sam's entire body tingled and his heart skipped a beat. "My verses!"

> My native country, thee,
> Land of the noble free,
>   Thy name I love;
> I love thy rocks and rills,
> Thy woods and templed hills,
> My heart with rapture thrills,
>   Like that above.
>
> No more shall tyrants here
> With haughty steps appear,
>   And soldier bands;
> No more shall tyrants tread
> Above the patriot dead;
> No more our blood be shed
>   By alien hands.
>
> Let music swell the breeze,
> And ring from all the trees
>   Sweet freedom's song.
> Let mortal tongues awake,
> Let all that breathes partake,
> Let rocks their silence break,
>   The sound prolong.

Because the tune was familiar and the printed program contained the words, the crowd gradually joined the children:

> Our fathers' God to Thee,
> Author of Liberty,
>   To Thee we sing.
> Long may our land be bright
> With freedom's holy light;
> Protect us by Thy might,
>   Great God, our King.

Thunderous applause erupted before the last phrase was finished.

"The whole crowd sang your verses," Lowell shouted as he greeted Sam after the program. "I predict that the song will sweep America."

"I had completely forgotten it," Sam replied modestly.

"I would like to introduce you to a young lady who

wants to meet the gentleman who composed those stirring verses," Lowell said. A young woman, whose blonde curls danced as she stepped forward, smiled up at Sam. "Mary White Smith, may I present Samuel Francis Smith."

"Your verses are beautiful," Mary Smith said, blushing. "I know they'll be sung many, many times." She turned to Lowell and said, "Thank you for introducing me to the man who made this Independence Day a memorable occasion." When she faced Sam again, her eyes were sparkling.

Sam extended his hand to Mary. She placed her gloved hand in his. "What is this strange feeling in my stomach," Sam wondered as he gazed at Mary. He had seen many pretty girls, but this one was— different. "I didn't realize I had written anything special," he said quietly. "I wrote what I felt in my heart. Then I forgot about it."

As the crowd thinned, people continued singing the new words to an old familiar tune.

"There you are!" Oliver Holmes shouted as he waved. "I've been looking for you." He wove his way through the crowd.

"Did you like the program, Oliver?" Sam asked.

Without answering Sam's question, Oliver blurted, "I hear that you wrote these verses." He pointed to the printed program. "Let me ask you, Sam, what does 'like that above' mean?" His voice took on an edge of criticism. "What does 'that' refer to?"

"That rapture," Sam replied.

"If I had been responsible for that line," Oliver said, "my heart would not 'with rapture swell like that above.' "

Sam let Oliver have the last word. He knew there was no sense arguing the point.

A few weeks after the celebration, Sam visited Lowell.

"Have you composed more lyrics that I can set to music?" Lowell inquired after he greeted Sam.

"Nothing new," Sam replied. "You already know about my missionary hymn, *The Morning Light is Breaking.*" Sam shifted his weight nervously from one foot to the other, and stroked his beard. "I have something other than verses on my mind today."

Lowell arched his eyebrows and peered over his spectacles.

"What's troubling you? It's my turn to help you, if I can."

"I have a question," Sam stammered, "—about the Independence Day celebration."

"Ah! Your verses!" Lowell replied. "They are sung everywhere now—schools, churches, public meetings."

"I wasn't referring to my verses," Sam said, looking down at his feet. His cheeks were bright red. "Oh, I'm pleased to know the verses are being used, but I came to ask your help about another matter."

"Come sit down," Lowell suggested, pointing to the chair across from his desk, "and tell me how I can help you."

Sam looked at Lowell and grinned. "It's that young lady, Mary Smith. I can't forget her. And not because her name is Smith."

Lowell nodded his head. "Well, my friend, there's not a lovlier girl around than Mary White Smith."

"Yes?" Sam inquired eagerly, pulling his chair closer to Lowell's desk.

"I've known Mary for a long time," Lowell said. "She lives in Haverhill, not far from Andover. Several of her ancestors were clergymen—so she knows what it's like to be part of a minister's family."

Sam blushed a deeper red. "What else can you tell me?"

"I've been told that her grandfather, Hezekiah Smith—a chaplain in the Revolutionary Army—was a close friend of George Washington." Lowell paused to think. "Since you are a poet, you probably know Mary's friend, John Greenleaf Whittier. He lives in Amesbury, near Haverhill."

Sam frowned. "Yes, I know him. Don't tell me that Mary is engaged to him!"

"No," Lowell replied. He laughed as he observed Sam's earnestness. They're just good friends. School classmates."

"Good," Sam said, drawing in a quick breath. "For a moment you had me worried."

"I don't think she's promised to anyone," Lowell said.

"Then you think it would be suitable for me to write to her?" Samuel's eyes crinkled around the corners, and he added, "—now that you've properly introduced us."

"Yes, of course." Lowell reached for his quill pen, wrote Mary's address on a scrap of paper, and handed it to Sam.

"Thank you, Lowell," Sam said, gazing at the address for a moment. He put it in his coat pocket. "Now, let's discuss music."

Sam settled back into his chair and listened as Lowell talked about the Sabbath School choir and his work. Eventually the conversation returned to Sam's verses.

"One reason the song has become popular is that the tune is familiar," Lowell explained. "Everyone can hum it; it's the words that are unforgettable."

"You're the music scholar," Sam said. "Tell me about the tune. Where did it come from?"

Lowell rocked back in his chair. "There are several legends. At Italian composer, named Lully, who was educated in France, wrote the music. Words to fit the tune were composed in 1686, and the song was used at the opening of a French convent. Because the melody was catchy, the great composer, Handel, asked permission of the nuns to make his own arrangement. Handel used English words with it and presented it as a new composition, dedicated to King George I of England. Handel titled it, *God Save the King*.

"I first heard the tune when I was a child," Sam added.

"A Danish clergyman, Heinrich Harries, composed words to honor the birthday of *his* king, Friederich Wilhelm of Germany. At once it became the German national hymn." Lowell paused and leafed through the papers on his desk. "Here's a copy of the English version," he said, and handed Sam a sheet of music.

"Another story claims that Dr. John Bull, a British music professor in the early 1500's, wrote the song for his friend, King James I of England. Some say that Dr. Henry Carey wrote both the words and music over a century after John Bull lived. Still another story says that it was composed for the birthday of King George II of England. So, you see, no one really knows the true story of *God Save the King*," Lowell concluded.

"It must have come to America with the colonists," Sam said, gazing at the music.

"Of course the early English colonists sang it," Lowell said. "In 1744 it appeared in a collection of music. After the American Revolution, other verses were set to the tune, such as *God Save George Washington*, and *God Save the Thirteen States*. It was even used when the Charlestown Bridge replaced the ferry from Charlestown to Boston," Lowell said with a chuckle. "I believe, Sam, that your Smith ancestors—or perhaps Mary's—operated the ferry."

"I'll find out for you," Sam said, grinning.

"We do not know whether these stories are legend or fact," Lowell said, "but we know the tune as *God Save the King*. Your verses bring to a fitting end the story of the song."

"I'm embarrrrassed at your praise, Lowell,"Sam said. "Oliver wasn't that impressed."

"I understand there is some criticism of the middle verse," Lowell admitted. "Some groups are not using it."

"So I've been told," Sam acknowledged. "The criticism is valid because if refers to the War of 1812 when Americans felt so bitterly toward the British. I'm sure that verse came from my own memories of cannons booming on Copp's Hill. I was only four years old at the time, but I'll never forget my terror."

Sam and Lowell sat quietly for a few minutes. In a low, strained voice Sam confided, "I wish I hadn't written that middle verse."

Lowell's eyebrows lowered in a frown. He chewed nervously at his lower lip. "I have to confess now that I have published your verses—all five of them—in the next edition of my musical journal, *The Choir*. I'm so sorry, Sam. I didn't tell you because I wanted to surprise you. If I had known how you felt about the middle verse, I never would have published it. The edition is just off the press, or I'd stop it now. Forgive me, Sam."

Sam touched his friend's arm. "Let's not worry about what cannot be changed. I appreciate your intentions, and I especially appreciate your friendship."

The 1832 edition of *The Choir* carried five verses titled *America*, set to the music of *God Save the King*. Lowell Mason had contributed the title to his country's national hymn.

The Smiths of Waterville, Maine

Sam returned to Andover for his final year of seminary with a new interest—Mary Smith. They wrote long letters to each other, and Mary's parents often invited Sam to visit their home. Haverhill, where Mary lived, was just a short distance from Andover, and before long, Sam was spending nearly every weekend with Mary's family.

In June, 1832, Sam graduated with high honors from Andover Seminary. He packed his belongings, said goodbye to Mr. and Mrs. Hitchings, and caught the stagecoach to Boston. He had important business to attend to—he needed a job.

After returning to Boston, one of the first persons Sam visited was Oliver. "I applied at the Baptist Church Headquarters to serve a church," Sam told him. "I was informed that not many churches can afford a full-time pastor, and that the big city churches are already served by older men with long-term contracts. I expect to begin in some small town."

"Are there any churches that will consider you now?" Oliver asked.

Sam sighed and shook his head. "It was disappointing to learn that it might be a long time before there's an opening. You know, Oliver, that I want to ask Mary to be my wife, but I don't think I should until I can offer her a decent future."

"What do you plan to do in the meantime?" Oliver asked. "Will you give up the idea of becoming a preacher?"

Certainly not," Sam said with confidence. "I'll wait for God to guide me. In the meantime I'll go on writing, and perhaps do some tutoring."

Mrs. Smith was delighted to have her son home again. Sam, however, was restless. He was in love with Mary, and wanted a home of his own. He visited Mary and her family as often as he could, and enjoyed long evenings talking to Mr. Smith while Mary sat quietly, watching every expression on Sam's face. She adored her Sam.

Sam knew it was the custom for a young man to ask permission from his sweetheart's parents before proposing marriage to her. He also knew that the Smiths approved of him and would agree to the proposal. But since he didn't have a regular income to support Mary, he continued to wait. Months passed by. Sam kept praying for a position where he could best serve God.

A year after Sam's graduation from Andover there came a glimmer of hope. He received a letter from Waterville, College, in Waterville, Maine, inviting him to become a professor of modern languages. About the same time, the little Baptist church in Waterville asked Sam to be interviewed for the position of pastor. "Finally," he thought, "I can ask Mary's parents about our marriage."

The stagecoach ride to Haverhill dragged on and on. Sam's stomach churned. He reached into his waistcoat pocket again and fingered the small gold engagement ring. It was safe. Even though certain the answer would be "yes," he practiced over and over the words he would use. "After all these years of 'declamations' and speaking, why am I nervous?" he asked himself. He shut his eyes and tried to rest. Pop! His eyes opened. "What if she says 'no'? She won't! She can't!"

Hours passed before the stagecoach finally lurched to a stop in the town square at Haverhill. It was late afternoon when Sam arrived at Mary's house. He picked nervously at his food during supper, eating only a few bites. Mary wondered what was wrong.

"Shall we go visit in the parlor?" Mr. Smith suggested. Everyone agreed and followed Mary's father across the hall.

"Mary," Sam whispered, tugging at her arm, "would you please allow me to speak to your parents alone for a moment?"

Mary blushed a deep red and nodded. She closed the parlor door behind Sam and returned to the kitchen.

Mary's parents seated themselves by the fireplace. Sam hesitated by the door, taking a deep breath. He forgot his carefully rehearsed speech and blurted out, "I—I love your daughter very much. May I marry her?"

Mr. Smith cleared his throat.

Mrs. Smith twisted her handkerchief.

Samuel's heart drummed in his ears as he studied their faces for an answer.

"Certainly we approve of you, Sam," Mr. Smith said slowly. "But—there's one concern I have. Can you provide a good living for our Mary?"

Sam's face blazed red up to his hairline with humiliation.

"I didn't mean to imply . . ." Mr. Smith quickly added. "That is, I know you have many journalistic endeavors, but do you have a steady position—a salary?"

"Not yet," Sam replied shyly, "but I have just received an offer to be Professor of Modern Languages at Waterville College, in Maine. I am also being considered as pastor of the Waterville Baptist Church and I expect the decision to be favorable. Between the two positions and my continued writing assignments, we should be able to live comfortably."

Mr. Smith stood and grasped Sam's hand. "I'll be happy to have you as a son-in-law."

Mrs. Smith, smiling broadly, kissed Sam's cheek. "I think we can safely trust our daughter to you, and with our blessing."

"Have you told Mary your good news—about Waterville?" Mr. Smith asked.

"No, sir. Not yet," Sam replied. "I wanted the surprise to be accompanied by your blessing. I wish I didn't have to take Mary so far away from you, but we will look forward to your visits. The railroad will soon be built that far."

Mr. Smith opened the parlor door and called loudly, "Mary! Sam wants to see you about an important matter."

Mary's face glowed as she entered the parlor. Mr. and Mrs. Smith left the room, and closed the door.

Sam gathered Mary in his arms, nestling his face against her soft, blonde curls. "Will you marry me, my darling?"

"Yes, Sam," she replied, pushing him back so that she could see his eyes. "I thought you'd never ask," she said playfully.

"Are you willing to risk life with a pastor?" Sam asked, holding her close. "You know that pastors often move from place to place. Sometimes they receive small salaries. I should also warn you that mission work on the other side of the world is appealing to me."

Mary's eyes sparkled like diamonds. "I'm willing," she answered.

Sam pulled Mary down beside him on the sofa and fumbled in his waistcoat until he found the gold ring. He slipped it on her tiny finger and kissed her. The engagement was sealed. "When would you like to become Mrs. Smith?"

"You know I'm a practical person, Sam," Mary said. "I think we should wait until you have a position in a church."

Sam grinned. "I have a surprise for you. I've been appointed Professor of Modern Languages at Waterville College. I begin in September. I'm also being considered as pastor of the Waterville Baptist Church. I should know about that soon."

Mary threw her arms around Sam's neck.

"The two positions will keep me busy," Sam warned, "and we may not have much time together."

"No matter where or how busy you are," Mary said, "I'll be glad to be with you. There's only one problem. All my life I was happy to be a girl so that I could change my common name of Smith when I married. Now you're asking me to be a Smith for the rest of my life." Sam and Mary laughed and held each other tightly.

Sam was ordained a Baptist minister on February 12, 1834. The simple, but dignified ceremony ended with the congregation singing four verses of *America*. Mary and her parents, and Sam's mother were there, as well as their special friends, Mr. and Mrs. Oliver Wendell Holmes.

On September 16, 1834, Mary and Sam were married in the Waterville Baptist Church. Mary looked like a princess in her white gown and veil. She glided down the aisle with her father as the church organist played. Sam watched proudly as she approached the altar. Her radiant face captured his heart again.

After the ceremony, the women of the church provided a delightful reception, complete with cake, in the festively decorated church hall. The Reverend and Mrs. Samuel Francis Smith left the building under a shower of rice. But there was no honeymoon, because Sam had classes to teach.

Sam and Mary moved into the church parsonage. Two evenings after their wedding, as they worked together washing the supper dishes, they heard a commotion on the front porch. Sam grabbed the kerosene lamp and threw open the door.

''For he's a jolly good fellow!'' the crowd of church members burst out in song.

"Come in," Sam said, inviting the singers into the parlor.

"You are all so kind!" Mary exclaimed when she saw that each person had brought a gift of food to stock the pastor's pantry. There were also cakes and cookies for the impromptu housewarming party.

"Sit down, and I'll bring tea."

The members of Waterville Baptist Church never forgot that evening of laughter and fun. They liked their new pastor and his bride.

Life settled into a routine for Sam and Mary, but in spite of their busy college and church schedules, there was always time for hospitality and entertaining. Sam and Mary often invited college students to their home and to church. They hosted parties and outdoor recreational activities. There were candy-pulls, sleigh rides in winter, and hay rides in summer. Many evenings were spent singing. *America* was always high on the request list.

Not all the Waterville College students knew of Sam's ability to quote from the Bible.

Each professor had to take his turn conducting morning devotions at chapel. At the end of Samuel's first week, he could hardly wait to tell Mary about it. With a twinkle in his eyes and a grin on his face, he hurried home on Friday.

"What a week!" Sam said with a laugh. "My first week of conducting chapel service ended this morning, and there are at least a handful of students who will never forget it."

Mary poured hot tea for Sam, and sat down to listen.

"When I went to the pulpit on Monday, the Bible wasn't there," Sam began. "I didn't think anything about it, but I quoted, from memory, a few Scripture verses. On Tuesday, the Bible was still missing, so I quoted a few more verses. On Wednesday, the Bible was still missing. By then I knew that someone was playing a trick on me. The students probably thought that if there wasn't a Bible, I would omit Scripture reading, and they'd get out of chapel sooner.'' Sam laughed so hard that tears rolled down his cheeks.

"I'm glad you see the funny side of everything," Mary said. "Now, stop laughing! I want to hear the rest of your story."

"On Thursday," Sam continued, shaking his head, "still no Bible. But I knew what to do. I quoted the entire twenty-second chapter of St. Luke—all seventy-one verses! Without comment, of course. On Friday morning—you'll never guess!"

"The Bible was back?" Mary asked, smiling.

"Of course!" Sam said, jubilantly. "I read several Scripture verses, as I normally would, and I made no other comment. But I can tell you that it was all I could do to keep from laughing. Now, Mary, do you think that will earn for me a reputation for being a good sport?"

"Yes," Mary said, giving Sam a hug, "and for having an extraordinary memory, too."

Maple leaves turned yellow and scarlet, and cold autumn wind carried them swirling to the ground. Sam and Mary prepared for their first holiday season away from their parents' homes. At Thanksgiving and Christmas, Sam's mother and Mary's parents journeyed to Waterville by train. Sam and Mary also invited students who were not able to go home for the holidays. Mary put all the extra leaves in the dining room table, and cooked endless amount of food. Her smile and good-nature told everyone how much she enjoyed being a hostess.

The Christmas holidays passed quickly, and it was

time for Sam's and Mary's parents to return home. On the way to the train station, Sam threw back his head and announced, "When you come to celebrate Independence Day, we'll have another celebration, too."

"A new song?" Mary's father asked.

Sam grinned. "We hope to add a name to the already long list of Smiths."

Tiny Mary White Smith, named for her mother, arrived in the late summer of 1835. She wasn't the only Smith baby for long. One year after Mary's birth, a sturdy boy, named Frank, joined the family. Baby Sarah arrived at the Smith parsonage in 1838, and two years later, Daniel Appleton White Smith joined his brother and sisters.

In September, 1841, when college opened, Sam was restless. Mary noticed it day after day.

"What's troubling you, Sam?" Mary asked one morning at breakfast. "I miss that twinkle in your eyes."

"Do adults get homesick?" Sam asked. "I'm homesick for Boston. This year when I saw my old Harvard friends of the Saturday Club at the Parker House Hotel in Boston, I knew I wanted to go home to live."

"It would be nice to be closer to our parents," Mary commented, squeezing Sam's hand, "especially since they are getting older."

The weeks passed. Sam became involved in teaching his classes, and Mary was busy caring for the children. It seemed like a normal fall until a letter for Sam arrived one day from Boston.

"Mary!" Sam shouted, waving the letter in the air. "Mary, I've been asked to be editor of *The Christian Review* journal."

Mary's eyes opened wide. "Does that mean we'll move to Boston?"

"Yes! Home!" Sam said, grabbing Mary's waist and twirling her around the kitchen table.

"Wait, wait!" Mary protested. "Could we live on that salary alone? Would you give up the things you love most—teaching and preaching?"

"I'd never give up preaching," Sam said. "There must be churches near Boston that can't afford a full-time pastor."

The kerosene lamp in the study burned late for many nights as Sam wrote letters inquiring about churches without pastors. Finally, an invitation to be interviewed arrived in Sam's mail.

One frosty November morning, Sam boarded the train for Boston. Thoughts spun in his head faster than the train wheels turned. He had already accepted the editorship of *The Christian Review*. He would just have to trust God to provide a church.

On November 14, 1842, Sam preached in the First Baptist Church in Newton Centre, just outside of Boston. When the worship service closed, the chairman of the pulpit committee asked Sam to wait while the members met to vote on their decision. Sam sat alone in the sanctuary, drumming his fingers on the pew. What was taking so long?

"Ahem!" The chairman cleared his throat, startling Sam. He jumped to his feet and faced the man. "Before making our final decision," the chairman said, "we would like to hear you preach again—soon. Can this be arranged?"

Sam's shoulders sagged. "I—I'm afraid not, sir," he stammered. "I can't leave my college classes again so soon, and the semester break is weeks away."

"Very well, Mr. Smith," the chairman stated crisply. "We'll bring the matter to the entire church membership next week. We'll send our answer to you by letter. Thank you for being with us today."

Sam shook hands with the committee members, and walked out into the chilly November air. His mood matched the gray sky. All the way to Waterville, he reviewed the morning's events. "Trust the Lord, trust the Lord," the rhythm of the train wheels seemed to repeat.

"Waterville!" the conductor called.

The sun had set, leaving a cold dusk to greet Sam. He trudged from the station to the parsonage. Mary and the children met him at the door with happy hugs and kisses. But Mary knew by his droopy shoulders that there was a problem.

He slumped into a kitchen chair, and put his arm around little Mary. The other children fought with one another to sit on his lap. He smiled at them, and gave each a warm hug.

"I can't wait another minute," Mary said, stamping her foot lightly. "Tell me what happened."

"The news will be the same after you sit down," Sam said, and managed a weak smile. "First, we'll thank God for my safe journey, and for my dear family, and our food." After all the little hands were clasped and the heads bowed, Sam prayed.

"Papa, you were gone so long," little Mary cried.

"I know, my dear," Sam said, smoothing her hair away from her face. "Cheer up. I'm not going away again for a long time."

"Sh-h-h, children," Mary cautioned gently as she served their supper. "Let your father tell us about his trip."

Sam took a mouthful of Mary's delicious supper and chewed thoughtfully for several seconds. "The congregation liked my sermon," he said. Mary nodded for him to continue. "At least they said so. But the committee asked so many questions, some rather personal. Then they met in the chapel for what seemed to me an eternity. When they returned, they reported that before they could give me a definite answer they wanted to hear me preach again, soon.'' Sam sat back and swallowed some steaming tea.

"Are you going back soon?'' Mary asked. She studied Sam's face, looking for signs of hopefulness, but all she saw were deep lines of worry stretched across his forehead.

"I said I couldn't leave my classes again,'' Sam answered with a discouraged sigh. "The chairman replied that the church would decide in a special meeting next week. They'll send the answer by letter.''

Mary put her hand over Sam's. "If they weren't considering you, they certainly wouldn't have asked you to return,'' she said, and squeezed his hand reassuringly.

"But why the delay?'' Sam asked, shaking his head.

"You'll know soon,'' Mary said. "A week is not a long time, Sam.''

A sudden smile broke through Sam's sober mood. "Maybe they think I only have one good sermon.'' Mary and Sam laughed, and the children giggled. "You know better than that, don't you?'' Sam inquired teasingly. They all nodded vigorously and clambered to give their father more hugs.

When the expected letter arrived a week later, Sam's hands shook as he tore it open. He couldn't wait, yet dreaded to know its contents.

"Yes? Yes?'' Mary was impatient, too, as Sam read the message. First he smiled, then grew sober, and finally frowned. "What is it? Tell me!'' Mary implored.

"They want me, but all they can pay is $450 for one year. Not much to support our family, is it?'' Sam handed Mary the letter, "Don't you frown, too,'' Sam teased as he watched Mary study it carefully. With the editorship, and some tutoring, maybe we can manage. What do you think?''

''I know you'll make the right decision, Sam,'' Mary answered as she linked arms with her husband.

That evening, when the children were in bed, Sam and Mary sat at the kitchen table and re-read the letter together.

''Do you remember that when we came to Waterville we received two offers at the same time? It's happening again!'' Sam exclaimed jubilantly. Then his mood changed. I can't understand, though, why the church has only asked me to come for *one* year.''

''You don't need to decide tonight,'' Mary said. ''Sometimes it's best to sleep on a matter before making a decision. Let's do something special to raise our spirits.''

Mary smiled secretively as she moved the iron teakettle to the front of the stove to heat the water. She reached into the cupboard, and slid the china cups aside. Deep in the cupboard, something silver glinted, even though it was dull with tarnish and disuse.

''Sam,'' she said, ''please reach the silver tankard for me—you know the one my grandparents gave us when we were married.''

''Why?'' Sam questioned, with raised eyebrows. ''We don't drink ale or beer.''

I'd like to look at it,'' Mary replied. ''I haven't taken it down for years. We could use it to drink tea. It's really beautiful when it's polished.''

Sam handed the tankard to Mary. After she polished it until it gleamed, she poured steaming tea into the tall tankard and handed it to Sam.

''My grandmother used to say that tea is the drink that cheers, but does not inebriate,'' Mary explained. ''I didn't know what she meant by 'inebriate' until I was grown.'' She laughed merrily. ''Go ahead, Sam, take a sip.''

"I'm not sure a Baptist minister should even have a tankard," Sam complained, "let alone drink out of one."

Mary shook her finger at Sam playfully. "That tankard is special. Originally it was given to my grandfather, Hezekiah Smith, by his friend George Washington. Mr. Washington had the initials 'HK' engraved on it, because it was a wedding present to Grandfather's bride, Hepzibah Kimball."

"For you, I'll drink tea from it," Sam said, winking at Mary. "Then please put it back in the cupboard. We don't want our new church to get the wrong idea about us."

The next morning, Sam wrote a letter:

Waterville, Maine, December 8, 1841

To the First Baptist Church and Society in Newton:

I have received your application, through Professor Ripley, to assume the duties of the ministry and pastorate among you for one year. I accept the compensation which you propose, although with the expectation that, if I should become permanently settled among you, it will be increased to at least $500.

I will commence my labors with you, Providence permitting, the first Sabbath in January, 1842.

S. F. Smith

Newton Centre

Weathervanes in Newton yielded to the piercing north wind on the first Sunday in January, 1842. Icicles hanging from rooftops glittered brightly as they caught the morning sun. The Smith children held hands and waited to cross the busy street with their parents. Never had they seen so many sleighs in one place.

As people in the sleighs passed, they waved at the children. Frost clung to the nostrils of the horses, and bells on their harnesses jingled crisply. Cold, sparkling snow creaked beneath the sleigh runners.

"All right, children," Sam said, and they all crossed the street together. In a few moments, the Smith family entered Newton Centre Baptist Church to begin Sam's new pastorate.

Newton began its history in 1639, when it was known as Cambridge Village. John Jackson, his wife, and fifteen children were the first settlers. Many Indians lived in the area, and Chief Waban permitted John Eliot to preach Christianity in his wigwam. Eliot established the first Christian community of Indians in the English colonies.

By 1645, ninety houses, occupied by one hundred thirty-five people, lined the village streets.

In colonial times, the Puritan church controlled both religion and government. Since Cambridge Village was considered to be an outpost, the laws and religious practices of the villagers were controlled by Puritan officials at Cambridge Town near Harvard Square. But it was difficult to travel that far to church, so Cambridge Village residents asked to have a separate church. In 1688, Cambridge Village became a town, called "Newtown." Seventy-five years later the name was shortened to "Newton."

In the early 1830's, railroads reached into the countryside and replaced the slow, rocking stagecoaches. In 1834, in spite of protests by Newton citizens, the railroad cut through the middle of town. The "iron horse" wheezed and puffed along its tracks. Farm land soon disappeared. Large, spacious homes sprang up on the wooded hillsides along the railroad track. Many wealthy Boston merchants moved to Newton because trains made it easy to travel into Boston for business and return to the country in the evening.

By the time the Smiths moved to Newton, it was a cluster of twelve small villages, sprawling along a large bend of the slowly moving Charles River. One village was named Waban, in honor of the old Indian Chief.

Sam purchased a large, rambling brown house on Center Street, only a few minutes' walk from the church. He kept his horse and buggy in a barn attached to the house.

"It's perfect," Mary said the day that the Smith family arrived in Newton. Her boot heels clicked on the hardwood floor as she hurried from room to room, inspecting her new home.

"See the building across the street?" Sam asked the children, pointing to a two-story wood structure. "That's the Rice School, which you will attend. I've already talked with the schoolmaster."

A few stores bordered the town common, which stretched from the school to the church. "The shops are close, too," Mary observed. "I'll be able to walk to do most of my shopping."

"The railroad station is just on the other side of the common," Sam added. "When I have to go into Boston on editorial business, I'll just hop on a train."

"Mother! Father! Come look!" Frank shouted through the kitchen door. His eyes sparkled with excitement as he pointed to the yard. "You picked the best house in Newton!" Outside, dozens of children were coasting on sleds down the snow-covered slope behind the Smith house.

The hill also proved to be a popular attraction in

the summer. Patches of wild flowers colored the slope, and at its base a tiny brook babbled over bright pebbles as it ran toward the Charles River.

Across the front of the Smith's house, tall wooden pillars supported a wide porch. Because Sam loved to watch and listen to children, he placed his study table by the front windows facing the school. On warm days, when doors and windows were open, Sam could hear children sing *America* as school opened for the day. Mary and Frank proudly sang the four verses of their father's song.

The Smith home was alive with activity and laughter. The children's friends loved to visit and be included in the family fun—hay rides, games, sleigh rides, skating, canoeing on the river, and picnicking in the woods. Young Frank and Mary were both old enough to help the smaller Smith children. Mary washed dishes and made beds. Frank filled the wood boxes and coalhods, and fed the horse.

The serious side of Smith family life was Sunday worship and family prayers. A big dinner followed Sunday worship, and because the Smiths enjoyed sharing their home with others, guests usually came for Sunday dinner. Sometimes the visitors would be a few of ''the boys'' from Sam's Harvard days, although most often it was the Oliver Holmes family. Sam's mother and Mary's parents were frequent guests, too.

One Sunday Sam called to his family and guests, ''Let's gather around the table.'' The Smith children took their usual places, guests were helped to their places, and everyone joined hands around the huge mahogany table in the low-ceilinged dining room. Beaming at the assembly of family and friends, Sam invited them to join in thanking God for His rich gifts.

When the blessing ended, everyone sat down. Mary

disappeared into the kitchen, and returned with steaming bowls and platters of food. She happily watched her family and guests enjoy their dinner. But she was careful not to catch Sam's eye, for fear she would laugh and spoil the wonderful surprise she had planned.

Little Mary helped clear the dishers, and Mary asked, "Would anyone care for more water?" She coughed lightly to disguise an excited giggle.

"I'll have another glass," Sam said. A few of the guests also requested water.

Mary returned from the kitchen with a gleaming silver "water pitcher," and poured water into Sam's glass. Sam's eyebrows shot up, but he didn't say a thing.

"What an unusual pitcher," Mrs. Waldrop remarked. "It looks a little like a tankard—"

"Yes, it does, a little," Mary responded quickly, with a smile. "It is quite old. It was a gift from George Washington to my grandfather's bride, Hepzibah Kimball."

After the last guest departed, Sam caught Mary in the dining room. "Water pitcher, heh?" he teased. "You gave Mrs. Waldrop—and me—quite a start."

"Don't you like it?" Mary asked. "I hoped I would surprise you with it."

"Oh, you surprised me, all right," Sam admitted. "let me look at it again."

"I had a jeweler attach a spout to grandfather's tankard," Mary explained, "so I could use it and enjoy it. It looks much nicer on my table than it does tucked away in some dark closet."

"Yes, it does," Sam agreed. "It suits you, and I think you should use it often."

"I will," Mary said, smiling merrily. The unusual "water pitcher" was present whenever the Smith's had company after that.

Sam stayed busy day and night. "The world has no use for a lazy man" was one of his favorite sayings. Evenings, when the children were asleep, Mary sat by Sam in his study. She darned and mended while she listened to Sam read something he had written. Often he asked for her criticism or advice.

After Sam had been pastor in Newton for six months, the church members decided that he should also be the church clerk. It would be his responsibility to record all church business in the big ledger book. One evening, after he recorded notes from the business meeting in the ledger, he leafed through the old records written before he had come to Newton.

"Hmm," he said aloud. "I think I've found the answer to the question we worried about before coming here. Remember? We wondered why I was asked for only one year."

"I still wonder about that," Mary replied, putting her mending aside to give Sam her full attention.

Sam read:

> November 14, 1841. A special meeting was held at the close of public worship, in reference to inviting Reverend S. F. Smith, now of Waterville, Maine, to become our pastor. He had been appointed Editor of *The Christian Review*, and was also willing to be pastor of some church in this vicinity. Having spent one Sabbath with us, he was requested to visit us again, to afford an opportunity to become further acquainted with him. He found it inconvenient, however, to make a second visit. In these circumstances, it was thought best to consult the church membership. As a result, it was unanimously voted that we invite Reverend S. F. Smith to become our pastor for one year.

Sam glanced at Mary for her reaction. "Here's the real answer."

It was thought desirable to state a limited time because there might be serious objections to providing permanent support for a person with whom we were not acquainted.

Mary giggled. "Seems as if they felt they might be getting a poor bargain, and wanted a way out if they didn't like you."

"Let me read more," Sam said:

December 1, 1841. Voted to give the Reverend S. F. Smith a call to become our minister for one year. Voted to pay him $450 for the term of one year.

Sam closed the ledger. "I wonder what will happen at the end of the year. It'll soon be here."

"What will we do if you aren't invited to stay?" Mary asked, soberly. "Soon we'll have another baby to add to our family."

"God will lead us," Sam replied.

When the year ended, the church officials asked Sam to meet with them. Sam stroked his beard nervously as he waited for the committee's decision.

The chairman stood and cleared his throat. "We are embarrassed because we can't increase your salary, as you requested," he said, peering down at the church ledger. "Contributions have been slow coming in. Under these circumstances, will you remain with us?"

Sam sighed inwardly. "I'll stay one more year," he said.

In 1843 Carrie Smith was welcomed into the family.

At the end of the church year in 1844, and again in 1845, the church treasurer reported that the money in the treasury barely covered expenses. Sam continued writing and accepting extra preaching and speaking engagements. He still edited *The Christian Review*. Somehow, the Smiths got along.

In 1849, Ewing Smith was born. The family was now equally divided—three boys and three girls. Sam knew it was time to find other sources of extra income.

"Would you object to having a bigger family?" Sam asked Mary, when Ewing was about six months old.

"We already have six children!" Mary exclaimed in surprise. "How many more can we afford?"

"After all these years," Sam scolded with a laugh, "don't you know when I'm teasing? I've been thinking about taking in several young men to board and tutor. Many ministers do that, and the money will help make up what the church can't pay. I'll teach our older children some of the same subjects that the young men are studying. No one can have too much education—boys or girls."

"It sounds like a good idea," Mary agreed, "but how soon?"

"Whenever you say," Sam replied. "You're the one who must settle the household arrangements. And I'll help you all I can."

The dining room became the classroom. Sam worked patiently with each student, but he was also strict. His students studied grammar and English literature. He assigned great passages of translations from Hebrew, Greek, and Latin. Often he read poetry to all the children, some written by their friend John Greenleaf Whittier, and another friend, Henry Wadsworth Longfellow. Sam ended each session saying, "School is over for today," but he knew they would all have to sudy to complete their assignments.

On holidays and civic occasions, an American flag flew from the Smith porch. Gradually, throughout the Newton villages, other families adopted the patriotic custom of displaying the flag.

Sam was continually asked to speak at civic functions, to write verses, or to participate in dedications and cornerstone-layings of new buildings. The four verses of *America* were a part of every celebration. In one of his speeches, Sam said, "Many people regret that we have adopted the music of Great Britain's national hymn, but I do not share that feeling. It is a symbol of union between Great Britain and America, and the two shake hands on common ground."

Many times, Sam's best thoughts for his speeches came to him during the night. He always kept a scrap of paper and a pencil on the table by the bed. Because he didn't want to disturb Mary's sleep, he sometimes scribbled in the darkness. One night, a particularly beautiful thought came to him. Without lighting the lamp, he wrote it down. The next morning, he discovered that the pencil point had been broken. His great inspiration was gone.

Sam liked people, and made many friends. No matter who came to his home, and no matter how often they came, day or night, he had time to spare. The family sometimes complained that visitors took up too much of his valuable time, but he replied, "Each person is important."

Once a month, Sam met "the boys" at the Parker House restaurant in Boston. At one of the reunions, Oliver Holmes offered this toast:

And there's a nice youngster of excellent pith;
Fate tried to conceal him by naming him Smith;
But he shouted a song for the brave and the free.
Just read on his medal, "My Country! 'Tis of Thee."

The Smiths became widely known in the greater Boston area—Sam as a lecturer, poet, teacher, and author, and Mary as a gracious and lovely hostess.

In 1854, Sam finished twelve years as pastor of the First Baptist church, and he felt it was time to discuss the future with Mary. "Twelve years," he said, and drew in a long breath. "That's a long time for any pastor to remain at one church. Perhaps I should resign."

Mary's eyes fluttered with shock. She studied Sam's face. It had a few wrinkles, but his eyes still sparkled. His hair was thinning, yet his beard was as full as ever. Even though he had never been sick, perhaps he wasn't feeling well.

"Leave Newton?" she asked, as if it were unthinkable.

"I'll never leave Newton," Sam stated firmly.

"But—" Mary said, her face pleading for an explanation.

"I've been thinking of resigning the church," Sam said, taking Mary's hands in his. "Then I'd be free to use all my time for other endeavors. I've been asked to become Secretary of the Baptist Missionary Union."

"Oh," Mary said, as relief swept her face. "That's wonderful. I know you've always wanted to be a missionary. You warned me many years ago that you might take us to the other side of the world."

"I haven't forgotten," Sam teased. "I still might take you away with me."

Mary's face darkened. "Will you have to travel away from home often if you accept the position with the Missionary Union?"

With his usual sense of humor, Sam replied, "Yes—to Boston every day. When the children are older, perhaps you and I will travel beyond Boston. But for now, I'll continue preaching in small churches that can't afford a full-time pastor. And I'll write and tutor. We still have children to prepare for college."

Mary smiled and squeezed her husband's hand. "Sam, you always have the right answers."

Fame and Honor

Sam traveled around the United States as Secretary of the Baptist Missionary Union. Everywhere he went—from Maine to Texas, from the top of Pike's Peak to the depths of Colorado's caverns—crowds and choirs honored him by singing *America*.

One day, when Sam was visiting Chicago, he went to the Board of Trade building to watch the exciting transactions. He sat quietly in the gallery, but someone recognized him. Suddenly, all trading stopped, and the traders burst into song: "My country, 'tis of thee. . . ." Sam stood and bowed.

"Come down!" men from the trading floor coaxed.

Sam shook his head, but the men were insistent. Finally several men climbed up to the gallery and escorted Sam to the trading floor. Then the traders and the gallery visitors joined in singing the remaining three verses. Thunderous applause followed.

Before the outbreak of the Civil War, Sam often spoke against slavery. During the Civil War his verses became more popular than ever. They were sung at recruiting stations, celebrations of victories, soldiers' funerals, and by women making bandages.

"Soldiers on battlefields and in hospitals sing *America*," General Howard reported at a reception for Sam in San Francisco. "The song is a tribute to their country."

From time to time, Sam looked through the tremendous collection of letters and newsclips he had received during the years that his words had grown in popularity. One day, in 1869, he found the original verses scribbled on the old envelope. Sam gazed at the envelope—especially the middle verse that had troubled him for so many years. He recalled the day that Lowell Mason returned that discarded scrap of paper. He also remembered Lowell's confession about the "surprise" printing of all five verses of the song in the 1832 edition of his music journal.

Sam pulled the desk drawer open and took out a pair of scissors. Snip-snap! He cut the envelope twice. He then pasted the two remaining pieces together. Without another thought, Sam tossed the middle verse into the wastebasket, and replaced the altered envelope among his mementos. He wouldn't be bothered by the verse again:

> No more shall tyrants here
> With haughty steps appear,
>   and soldier-bands;
> No more shall tyrants tread
> Above the patriot dead;
> No more our blood be shed
>   By alien hands.

Sam never publicly explained why, or when, he destroyed the middle verse.

Although Sam was grateful for honors and praise of his work, nothing pleased him as much as his children. He had educated them so well that both

Daniel and Mary entered directly into their
sophomore year of college. Daniel graduated from
Harvard in 1859 and entered Newton Theological
School in Newton Centre. From there he graduated
in 1861. That same year he married a lovely southern
girl whose name was Sarah.

One day Daniel paced up and down in front of the
Newton Centre train station while waiting for the late
afternoon train. He glanced at the station clock.

"Late," he mumbled. "Of all days, why does the
train have to be late today?" He sat on the bench but
his feet tapped the pavement nervously. He decided
to walk again. No one but his wife Sarah knew what
was in his heart. He wanted his father to hear it first.

Finally, the low rumble of the steam engine broke
the silence. Daniel gazed down the track, waiting to
see the cloud of steam that would announce the train's
arrival. The great engine groaned as it eased into the
station, and hissed to a halt. Daniel glanced quickly
at each person who emerged from the cars. He tipped
his hat to the familiar faces, and shifted his weight
anxiously from one foot to the other.

"Where is he?" Daniel wondered impatiently.

"Looking for someone?" Sam asked softly over
Daniel's shoulder.

"Father!" Daniel exclaimed, turning and grasping his father's hand. "I—uh—I—" He wanted to
blurt out the surprise, but now he couldn't find the
right words.

"You look hungry, son," Sam said, giving Daniel's
ribs a good-natured poke. "I happen to know where
there's a good place to have supper. It's nearby and
has a good parlor where men can do some serious
talking."

Daniel dropped his head and smiled. "Sarah's
already at the house helping Mother prepare supper."

"Let's go," Sam said, pulling Daniel's arm. "I'm starving."

The two men crossed the common. Daniel listened as his father told him about his day's work at the Baptist Missionary Union.

"There's so much work to be done overseas," Sam lamented, "and not nearly enough young people who are willing to go."

"That's what I came to the station to tell you," Daniel said quietly. "You know that I was disappointed when the Union Army refused to admit me because of my weak heart. I very much wanted to be a patriotic citizen. But Sarah and I still believe the Lord guides our lives."

Sam looked at his son with anticipation.

"Do you remember the Burmese student who attended Newton Theological School years ago, when I was about fourteen?" Daniel asked. "You know how much I enjoyed talking with him about his country and his people. He asked me to come and work among his people someday. Sarah and I believe that day has arrived."

Sam stopped and faced his son. His eyes brimmed with joyful tears. "I was never able to fulfill my dream to be a missionary," he said, gripping Daniel's shoulder. "So I have prayed that one of my children would take the gospel to a distant and needy land. I'm proud of you, Daniel."

In 1863, Daniel and Sarah traveled to the other side of the world as missionaries to Burma. Soon after they arrived, they met the Burmese man who had lived in America.

"I've come," Daniel told him.

Mary and Sam spent quiet evenings together now. The children were all grown and had left home to earn their own livings. Samuel's mother had died. There was nothing more to keep them from traveling outside the United States.

Mary often walked to the railroad station to meet Sam as he returned from Boston. One humid August afternoon, as she sat on the bench at the railroad depot, she fanned herself to dry the perspiration on her forehead.

When Sam stepped off the car steps, Mary rushed to greet him. He seemed unusually spry. She sensed that he had something special to tell her.

Sam linked Mary's arm in his as they slowly climbed the ramp to the street. His first words were, "Mary, it's almost time for our forty-first wedding anniversary. I've planned a celebration that only you and I will observe. Several years ago, I promised to take you traveling with me. Remember?"

"I remember," Mary replied, "But we've been so busy with our children and the students, there hasn't been time for us to go."

"We don't have to stay home any more and let moss grow under us," Sam said.

"What kind of traveling do you have in mind?" Mary asked.

"We're going to the British Isles and France. Do you think you can bear to be that far from Newton and the children?"

During Sam's recital of these plans, Mary's mouth opened wide and her eyes sparkled in excitement. "Of course I can!" she exclaimed. "When do we leave?"

"On our anniversary, September 16," Sam replied, squeezing her arm close to his. "I'll be combining business with pleasure. I will visit churches and colleges. We will meet many persons with whom I have corresponded for a long time. I shall write articles and reports to be published in our missionary journal."

By this time Sam and Mary had reached their

home. Sam opened the front door and said, ''Better start packing.''

As Sam helped Mary clear the supper dishes that evening, he said, ''Let me show you our itinerary.'' Later that evening, Sam and Mary huddled together studying travel brochures and maps.

''Have you told the children?'' Mary inquired.

''Yes, and they urged me to go,'' Sam replied.

On September 16, Sam and Mary sailed for England. There were gone a full year.

When they returned in 1877, Boston had a problem that needed Sam's attention. Progress threatened to destroy the Old South Meeting House. Sam, along with some of his old classmates and friends worked to save the building where the Boston Tea Party was organized. At a rally, Sam appeared with such celebrities as Ralph Waldo Emerson, Julia Ward Howe, Dr. James Freeman Clarke, and of course, Dr. Oliver Wendell Holmes. Each pleaded with the crowd to save ''Old South.'' Mrs. Howe explained how she wrote the *Battle Hymn of the Republic*. Oliver Holmes told about writing the famous poem that saved *Old Ironsides*, and Sam described how he composed the verses of *America*. ''Old South'' was saved from destruction.

Around the World

In 1880, Sam and Mary, now seasoned travelers, were ready for another adventure. Daniel had written, "There's no reason for you not to come to Burma and to tour Europe, too, With Father's knowledge of languages, it will be easy. Besides, we would love to have you visit Burma to see us and to see what has been accomplished for God's kingdom."

Sam and Mary didn't need coaxing to plan a two-year schedule. Sam would write letters home to the children, and to the missionary headquarters in Boston.

When Sam and Mary climbed aboard the train at South Station headed for New York, a huge crowd was gathered to see them off. The Smith children—Mary, Frank, Sarah, Carrie, and Ewing—had each written letters for their parents to deliver to Daniel and his wife Sarah. Many people shouted greetings for the Smiths to take to friends in Europe. As the train crept out of the station, the crowd sang *America*. In a few hours, Sam and Mary walked up the gangplank of the steamship that would carry them to their first foreign destination—London.

The trip across the Atlantic was uneventful. Sam and Mary enjoyed a longer visit in England than they had planned, because all the steamships headed for the Orient were full. Finally, on October 23, 1880, they boarded the steamer, *Tenasserim*, and began their long voyage to the other side of the world. Hand in hand, Sam and Mary stood at the railing and watched the Glasgow seaport fade in the distance.

"I'm looking forward to seeing Daniel and Sarah," Sam said, squeezing Mary's hand. "And I'm especially anxious to see how God's kingdom is prospering where they are in the Orient."

The *Tenasserim*, plunged through the ocean waves along the coast of France and through the Strait of Gibralter into the warm waters of the Mediterranean Sea. This ship was one of a fleet of five steamships belonging to the British and Burma Navigation Company. Each made about three trips to Rangoon, Burma, every year.

Among the twenty-four passengers were eight new missionaries accompanying Sam to Burma. One of these was a young man named Myat Tway. Myat, who was a member of the Karen tribal people of Burma, had been studying in America for five years. Now he was returning to preach and to teach to his people in Burma.

The passengers developed a daily routine. During the days, they studied, read, and wrote letters. In the evenings, they gathered together to practice speaking various languages, and to sing and talk. The passengers begged the returning missionaries to tell more stores about Burma. Sam enjoyed talking with the young missionaries as much as he liked walking around the deck to watch the mighty sea.

Every time the ship docked, Sam mailed letters to his family and reports to his office. In one letter he wrote:

> The voyage from Glasgow thus far has been as favorable as could have been reasonably expected. Sometimes the sea has been unfriendly. Many days, however, have been balmy and sweet, like a beautiful breath of summer, to those whose New England origin would lead them to expect at this date the sharpness of late autumn and early winter.
>
> Many objects of interest varied the tedium of the voyage. The ever-changing aspects of nature, the glorious sunsets, the brilliant moonlight, the occasional passing of vessels, islands and headlands and lighthouses from time to time coming into view and then vanishing again, the recognition of geographical points, hitherto having only a shadowy existence on maps, now seen face to face; the rainbow, the wonderful clouds, the glorious phosphorescent ocean—all served to relieve the monotony of sea and sky and far-away horizon.

While Sam enjoyed most of the voyage, he especially liked times when the steamer anchored at a port long enough for the passengers to get off and wander the streets of new and strange cities.

The gangplank dropped with a thud on the dock at Port Said at the entrance of the Suez Canal. Sam and Mary joined several of the travelers and hurried onto shore, anxious to explore the Egyptian city.

"Oh, my legs!" Mary exclaimed as she wobbled and fell against Sam. "I feel like I'm still rocking over the waves on the ship."

"We'll walk slowly," Sam said, taking Mary's arm. "Pretty soon we'll get our 'land-legs' back."

Sam, Mary, and their ship friends wandered through the narrow dirt streets lined with merchants hawking their wares. Men in turbans and baggy pants came out from under colorful canopies to show the travelers brass vases and coffee urns, baskets, and bright stips of cloth. Women wore veils that completely covered their faces. Narrow strips of lace allowed the women to see out, but the travelers could not see the women's eyes. Tattered beggars slept on piles of rubbish in the alleys.

As they returned to the steamer, they saw a few trees with green leaves in a garden, but everywhere else there was only sand and burning sunlight. A man with a dark Egyptian face passed them, leading a heavily burdened camel.

"Europe is far behind us," Sam commented quietly.

The *Tenasserim* left Port Said and passed through the Suez Canal into the Red Sea.

"Where do you suppose God parted the sea?" Mary asked as she joined Sam at the deck railing.

"I was just wondering the same thing," he said, and pointed toward the vast desert and barren hills on the shore. "Just think of the great people who have traveled through this country. Joseph probably came this way after his brother sold him to Egyptians. His whole family came later. And Moses talked to God out in that desert somewhere."

"Yes," Mary said, as she scanned the rugged landscape. "I can picture Mary and Joseph and baby Jesus fleeing across those rocky hills to Egypt, too."

"Can you imagine the millions of Israelites camping alongside this sea?" Sam asked, shaking his head. "They wandered for forty years out in that wasteland. Manna fell there to provide them food."

"Parts of the voyage have been hard for me," Mary said, slipping her arm through Sam's. "But looking at this place where God led His people, I feel refreshed. I know He's leading us, too."

The steamer left the east coast of Africa and sailed into the lonely Indian Ocean. The passengers seldom saw another ship, and wondered if they were alone in the world. The sun blazed in the sky and the temperature soared. The pasengers were grateful when clouds shielded them from the sun's rays. On cloudy days, they saw bright bursts of lightning and colorful rainbows in the distance.

Early one morning Mary asked her husband, "Do you know what day this is?"

Sam thought for amoment. "Why, it's Thanksgiving Day!" he exclaimed. "It's awfully hot, though. And I suppose it's snowing in Boston today."

"I can't honestly say whether I prefer tropical heat or New England cold," Mary said, fanning herself, "but I wouldn't enjoy baking pumpkin pies in this climate."

"How should we celebrate?" Sam wondered.

"I can assure you that there won't be turkey and cranberries for supper," Mary said with a laugh.

"Let's gather the other passengers and sing some hymns today," Sam suggested. "We don't need special food to show God that we are grateful."

All day the *Tenasserim* steamed along the shores of Ceylon (now called Sri Lanka). Instead of their usual routines, the passangers sang and observed the beautiful landscape. Green mountains seemed to pile up in back of one another, creating a background for the white buildings that studded the shore. As Thanksgiving Day faded following a brilliant sunset, Ceylon disappeared from view.

The last day of the voyage finally dawned on December 1. Mary and Sam busily packed their trunks and got ready to leave the steamship.

As the ship approached Rangoon, green waves of the Bay of Bengal gradually turned into muddy waters of the Gulf of Martaban.

"There's Elephant Point, "Sam called to Mary. "See the tall, stone pillar? And there's the lighthouse Daniel said to watch for. We're at the mouth of the Rangoon River."

Passengers gathered at the railings to gaze at the strange Oriental sights. There were coconut palm trees, rice fields, yoked water buffaloes, straw covered huts built on stilts, and golden pagodas where the Burmese worshiped their gods.

The steamer dropped anchor in Rangoon, a city of Oriental beauty, yet troubled by filth and poverty. Passengers eagerly searched the crowd on the pier for familiar faces. Hundreds of people were there, waving hats and handkerchiefs and throwing kisses.

"Stay with us," Sam told the new missionaries. "We don't want to lose you in the crowd."

"Father!" Daniel shouted and waved. At last the four Smiths were together again, hugging, kissing and talking at the same time.

Sam held Daniel at arm's length and gazed at his face. "It's good to see you, son, " he said. His eyes shone with pride.

"I want you to meet some special friends," Daniel said, and nodded toward a group of about thirty young Karen students. "I had to bring them. They begged me to suspend classes today so that they could help welcome my mother and father from America."

Sam grasped each student's hand warmly. "You aren't strangers," he told them, "but friends. Daniel has written to us about you." The students grinned and graciously bowed to welcome the American visitors to Burma.

Rangoon

Soon after Sam and Mary arrived in Burma, Daniel arranged to have members of various churches come for tea. The first evening, men and women from the Burmese church came. Some were dressed in poor clothing, others were adorned by fine jewelry and rich robes. Daniel introduced each one to his parents, and told them a little about how that person had become a Christian.

"This is the widow of Ko En," Daniel explained, presenting an old woman whose homely face glowed with joy and gentleness. "Her husband helped the famous missionary, Dr. Judson, translate the Bible into Burmese. Now she continues to help with the gospel work."

A woman with refined manners stepped forward. She urged her four-year-old son, who was dressed in Chinese clothing, to bow to the American guests.

"Her husband is Chinese," Daniel explained, "but he allows her to worship and to give liberally to the Christian church here. She provided the money needed to build the bell tower on the chapel."

A Burmese man who was an official for the British government greeted Sam and Mary in English. After the American guests had spoken, the man approached Sam again and said. "That speech felt me." Sam could see that the man was a sincere Christian. Then the man turned to Mary, and gestured at her head. "Majestic," he said, referring to her silvery curls.

Another young man spoke with Sam. "I am employed by the British at the Post Office," he said. "I earn 150 rupees a month, but I'm considering becoming a missionary preacher. I would only earn 20 rupees a month, but to serve the Lord is worth the cut in pay."

The missionaries served their American and Burmese guests tea and simple refreshments. At the end of the evening, they sang a hymn. Daniel chose *The Morning Light Is Breaking*, which he had translated into the Burmese language.

"My father wrote the words to that song," he told the people.

One man commented with awe, "To think that I have sung that hymn so many times without knowing that you were the author."

On the second evening a similar gathering took place. About seventy Karen men and women came. They cordially introduced themselves, in American fashion, by shaking hands and telling Sam and Mary their names.

Daniel explained, "Only a few years ago the Karen people had no written language, no Bible, and no hope. The Burmese looked down on them as inferior people, and forced them to live in the mountains and jungles. Then missionaries came, and told them about Jesus. They helped the Karens develop a written language and schools for all ages. Many of my students in the seminary will become teachers and preachers of the gospel."

One of the guests was a lawyer who practiced law in the Rangoon courts. He spoke perfect English. Presenting him, Daniel said, "Father, I'd like to introduce you to a fellow poet. He writes hymns, and his little daughter sings."

"Could we hear a song?" Sam suggested. The man and the child were delighted to perform for the American visitors.

Daniel's face beamed as he drew another man toward his father. "I am proud to present Dr. Sau Tay, the head native teacher in our seminary." Dr. Tay shook Sam's hand warmly.

"Father, do you remember, when I was about fourteen, that I met a young Karen student at Newton Theological School? He asked me to promise that when I grew up I would come to Burma to help him teach his people. Dr. Tay is that young man. I couldn't do without him at the seminary."

"Although I am not a young man any more," Dr. Tay replied, "I am happy to work with your son, who has fulfilled that long-ago promise. And, Dr. Smith, I so well remember singing your wonderful words, "My country, 'tis of thee." Did you know that it is our national hymn, too? The same musical measure, but with Karen words. We often use it for patriotic gatherings."

Sam studied the Karen man's face, wrinkled with age but glowing with joy. "I remember you," he said. "We know that you had a great influence on Daniel's decision to become a missionary. We're grateful to you."

Sam called Mary to his side and introduced Dr. Tay. "You had Sunday dinner with us often," she recalled. "It was always a pleasure to hear your stories about Burma."

When tea was served, many of the older Karen

people sat on mats on the floor, which was their custom. They had never held tea cups before, but no one spilled a drop.

Telugu and Tamil people attended the third tea party. They had come from the opposite coast of India to work as servants and coolies in Rangoon. They formed their own church with a Telugu pastor and worshiped in their own language.

"When these people become Christians," Daniel explained, "they like to adopt Biblical names." Sam and Mary were introduced to John and Abraham, Elizabeth and Naomi, and many others with familiar names.

After tea, the people sang hymns, but unlike the other evenings, the Tamil and Telugu music was strange to Sam and Mary's ears—not at all like American hymns translated into another language.

When the guests had gone home, the four Smiths stayed up late talking about the people and the changes that had taken place since Dr. Judson began the work seventy years before. They reminded themselves of those hard early days. It had been against the law for people to adopt Christianity, as it was the religion of "foreigners." So Dr. Judson worked for six years before he saw his first convert. After that, as belief in Christ spread, so did terrible persecutions.

"I'm glad that the people now have freedom to choose what to believe and how to worship," Daniel said. "Dr. Judson would be pleased with the progress the Lord has allowed."

Sarah carried the last tea cups to the kitchen. "Now that you've met some of the people," she said, "it's time to show you the city where they live. Tomorrow we will begin to tour Rangoon."

Rangoon, the most prominent city of Burma, looked a little like England, with an Oriental flavor.

When Burma came under British rule, Rangoon was redesigned. Old paths and streets were ripped up, and idol monuments were torn down and crushed to make hard, compact roads.

The city was laid out in squares, with broad avenues bordered with shade trees. Many streets were one hundred feet wide. Other native business avenues were narrow and congested with people buying and selling from colorful stands.

Watering carts lumbered along the streets spraying mist to keep the dust down. Kerosene lamps from New York City lighted the main streets at night. When Sam mailed letters, he found that the corner mailboxes looked just like the ones in Boston.

As the Smiths walked down the streets, they passed many places where people worshiped. Some were Christian churches, but others were Hindu temples, Jewish synagogues, Muslim mosques, and Chinese joss-houses. On streets lined with poor native houses made of posts, mats, and slats, there were many small pagodas. People burned incense as they worshiped countless gods which they had made with marble and cement. Priests led the worshipers who knelt and touched their heads to the ground.

People jostled one another on the crowded sidewalks. Most of the men wore turbans, although some liked British hats. Even the poorest people wore some kind of head covering because of the sun's glaring heat.

"The people look like a rainbow," Mary exclaimed.

"White and red are the favorite colors," Daniel said, "but you will see all kinds of clothing: turbans, pants, skirts, and even simple waist-cloths in an endless variety of colors."

"Pink, blue, orange, yellow, green," Mary said indicating the people on the street. "And look, there's **a man wearing calico!**"

"People from all over Burma and India and the Orient flow into Rangoon," Daniel explained. "Each group brings its own customs and dress."

"It was hard for me to get used to how little some of the people wear," Sarah admitted. "See the children playing in the alley? They don't have on one stitch of clothing. But if you look carefully, you'll see a fine silver bracelet on each of their ankles."

"It's so hot and dusty here," Daniel explained, "that heavy clothing is uncomfortable. The workers wear 'tow-cloths' that scarcely cover them."

"Let's go listen to that street preacher for a few minutes," Sam suggested. "He's drawing quite a crowd."

The preacher stood barefoot on a platform. Sam and Mary couldn't understand many of the words, so Daniel translated. He was talking about Jesus. When the man finished his sermon he picked up his small platform and walked through the crowd talking to people individually.

Sam noticed how dust rose up around the man's bare feet as he walked away. "Bare feet are as acceptable here as well-brushed boots are in Boston," Daniel explained.

Since Daniel could not leave his work at the seminary, Sam and Mary traveled without him to other cities as they continued their tour of Burma.

A Meeting
in the Forest

In the city of Bassein, Sam awoke early one morning and decided to do some exploring by himself. He wandered through the narrow streets and watched women preparing the morning food on charcoal fires. He came to a fine pagoda and walked inside. The walls shone with gold. Huge grim lions, carved from stone, stared coldly at him as they guarded a statue of Buddha. Sam heard the shuffle of feet outside the pagoda door. An old woman with a sincere but troubled face entered and dropped to her knees.

The woman reached up and took a tray containing six or seven small dishes of food from her head. She bowed down on her knees and elbows and offered the food to the Buddha. She mumbled a few words in her own language and poured some rice into a saucer. She slowly rose to her feet and carried the saucer to a shelf which hung from a tree that grew in the pagoda. She poured the rice onto the shelf as an offering to the "nat," whose spirit she believed lived in the tree.

Suddenly there was a flutter of black wings as hungry crows swooped down to devour the rice. A few grains dropped to the ground. Skinny dogs, who hung around the pagoda, snarled at each other as they fought over the crumbs.

Sam watched sadly while the woman returned to mumble prayers to the Buddha. She was trying to win enough merit to improve her situation in her next life. She probably hoped to return as a man.

Another worshiper entered the pagoda, and he spoke to the woman. She looked up from her prayers and nodded at the man. They knelt together to pray before the stone statue, but often stopped to talk and laugh. Sam was amazed at how lightly they took their worship.

Sam and Mary traveled beyond the cities of Burma into the forests. On the first leg of their inland journey, they rode a railroad. The train wasn't as ornate as American trains, but it made the trip through the dense jungle easily and quickly. A man met them at the Thonzai station with an oxcart drawn by two bulls. In this they rode to the local missionary's home.

Later they made a trip with Daniel to attend a special meeting in a small Christian village in the forest. First, they traveled by steamship to the Tavoy River. Then at the edge of the river Daniel announced, "Here is our next boat." Sam and Mary glanced at each other with startled expressions.

The boat was carved from the trunk of a large tree, and was about thirty feet long. Near the middle, was a thatched roof on poles, which could provide passengers shelter from the hot sun during the day, and the heavy dew at night. Under the roof, the boat was about five feet wide.

"We expected to have some adventures on our trip," Sam said, "and I'm sure this boat ride will be one of them." He took Mary's hand and helped her climb into the boat that bobbed at the river's edge.

Mary straightened her skirt and sat in the shade of the thatched roof. "It may be primitive," she commented, winking at Daniel, "but it's reasonably comfortable."

"I hope you will still think so when we arrive at Shatapee tomorrow afternoon," Daniel said.

After the passengers were boarded, a dozen Christian Karen young men pushed the boat into the river, and took their places to row or to steer. A second boat joined them for the journey.

"How many people do you expect will attend the meeting?" Sam asked Daniel.

"We've received letters saying that twenty-one Karen churches will send representatives," Daniel replied. "Many other churches have responded to our invitation, but they can't send delegates because their journeys would be too difficult. They'd have to cross treacherous streams or walk through forests filled with wild animals. For others, it's just too far. However, their letters telling about the Christian work in their areas will be read at the meeting."

"How many days will we be there?" Mary asked. She brushed away insects and fanned herself to keep cool.

"We'll be there four days," Daniel answered, "but many of the Karens will stay for weeks. Because it is now January and the rice harvest is over, they aren't in any hurry to return home."

The boats skimmed easily over the muddy jungle river. Once in a while, when a boat jolted to a halt on an unseen shoal, one of the oarsmen leaped into the water to free it. At other times, strong currents seized the boats, making them impossible to steer. Then young men eagerly plunged into the water to swim beside the boats and guide them to safety.

The passengers finally setled down to enjoy the long voyage. The flat, muddy riverbank framed the edges of dense jungle. Sometimes in the distance, the travelers could see towering mountain peaks with higher ranges rising behind them. Strange, Oriental trees rose up from the jungle floor.

Occasionally, the river widened and the only sound the travelers heard was the splash of oars. When the river narrowed, they could hear children's voices. But they rarely saw any children because their villages were hidden in the dense forest.

As darkness came, jungle noises seemed to close in around the boats. Birds and animals called with eerie squawks and screeches, while insects hummed incessantly in the evening air. Splashes in the river marked a fish leaping to catch his supper or animals quenching their thirst on the banks. The oarsmen suddenly turned the boats toward the river bank, and anchored them.

"We'll rest here for about four hours," Daniel explained.

When the passengers awoke, sunlight sparkled on the heavy dew dripping from the trees. The boats were already underway.

At about noon, they came to where the river flowed through a hilly section and sheer cliffs rose straight up from the banks. The oarsmen turned the boats sharply against the current, and into a hidden cove.

Happy shouts filled the air as dozens of Karens crowded along the riverbank to greet the guests. After the oarsmen pulled the boats to shore and secured them, numerous hands reached out to help the passengers climb safely up the steep and slippery bank.

"Where do all these people live?" Mary asked. "I don't see a single house."

"There are many houses in the village," Daniel said, "but they're hidden by thick vegetation. We're going to stay in the chapel. Other visitors will sleep and cook in booths set up especially for the meeting."

The chapel had been divided by curtains into small rooms for the special guests from Rangoon. Sam and Mary soon made themselves at home, and then walked with Daniel to explore other parts of the village.

Not far from the chapel was a temporary structure for the meetings. Sam and Mary noticed that groups were preparing and eating their midday meal in tent-like booths. Each church group had brought its own food and cooking utensils.

The deep, rich sound of a gong vibrated through the forest. The Karens left their booths and walked toward the meeting hall. Men, women, and children were dressed in their colorful holiday clothing. Silk turbans of red, white, yellow, green, and even plaid adorned men's heads, and contrasted with the women's black, shining, uncovered hair.

"They look like a moving flower garden!" Sam explained.

"The rest of the world seems shut out, doesn't it?" Daniel remarked.

Sam nodded in agreement as he gazed at the tall green hills and the dense jungle all around them. Even the sunlight had difficulty penetrating the leafy canopy above their heads.

As the first prayer meeting closed, a group of young Karens stood in front of the chapel in the light of the full moon and sang several hymns in their own language. The last one was, "My country 'tis of thee . . . ."

The meetings progressed over the next few days

with delegates making resolutions and discussing
problems in their churches. Daniel, as well as Karen
men, preached, and several men were examined for
baptism and ordination. Sam was impressed with the
business of the church in the jungles of Burma. He
and Mary might even have forgotten that the meetings
weren't in America except for the occasional crashing
of bamboo in the forest nearby as an elephant roamed
past looking for his dinner.

Sunday dawned bright and beautiful, with morning sun glowing through the trees. After a worship
service in the bamboo meeting hall, everyone walked
down to the calm cove of the river for a baptismal
service. As each new believer was baptized, the
missionary called out, ''Lord, it is done as thou has
commanded.'' The missionaries and Karens sang in
the Karen language, and Sam joined in in English
on ''Praise God from Whom all Blessings Flow.''

Following the baptism was still another service, this
time for ordaining two new pastors. One was Sau
Plaipau, a grandfatherly man wearing an orange silk
turban. His wise and solemn face made Sam think
of Socrates. The other man was young Sau Wah, who
was also dressed festively, yet looked solemn. The missionaries and Karen pastors laid their hands upon the
two men's heads and prayed. Sam wished that friends
of missions in America could have seen this ceremony.

Early the following morning, Sam and Mary
climbed into the boat for their return trip. They felt
as if they were leaving friends. Karens waved goodbye from the riverbank and Sam and Mary waved
to them until the current carried the boat around a
bend.

India and Ceylon

It was a tearful goodbye for all four of the Smiths: Sam and Mary, Daniel and Sarah. Mary wiped tears from her eyes as she and Sam leaned over the ship's railing to shout last minute reminders of their love. She held tightly to Sam's hand as the *Oriental* slowly left the shore.

"It's so difficult to leave," Mary sobbed, "when we know it will be a long time before we see them again."

"I know," Sam replied, giving Mary a hug, "but now we'll be able to picture in our minds where they live. And we know how good the native people are to them." As the steamship moved out of Rangoon harbor, Sam encouraged Mary. "Let's look forward to meeting new friends in Calcutta."

"I suppose we should," Mary said, "but I wish Daniel and Sarah could travel with us."

The voyage from Rangoon to Calcutta took four days. As the sun set on the fourth day, the steamship anchored at the mouth of the Hoogly River, about

ten miles from Calcutta. The following morning, the
ship chugged up the river.

In Calcutta, there were no piers where the ship
could dock. Passengers climbed down into small boats
that ferried them to shore. Reverend Norris, pastor
of the Baptist Chapel in Calcutta, met Sam and Mary
and welcomed them. "I'm sorry that my wife couldn't
come with me to greet you," he apologized. "She
hasn't been feeling well."

"We understand," Sam said. "We're just grateful
that you were able to come. It would be difficult for
us to find our way around Calcutta without help."

Sam and Mary joined their host in a carriage and
soon arrived at the Norris' home.

Mrs. Norris met them at the door. Three little girls
giggled and hid behind her skirts. "Come out, girls,"
she said, "and meet our guests from America."

The Smiths and Norrises settled on the shady porch
and drank tea.

"It's good to hear news from America," Mrs.
Norris said after listening to Sam and Mary talk about
their home and travels. "We lived in Bristol, England
for a while. I liked it there."

"Are you finding life in Calcutta difficult?" Mary
asked. "I know that it would be hard for me to adjust
to this hot weather. In Newton it is probably snowing
today."

"I'm glad to be able to serve the Lord," Mrs.
Norris replied, "but living in India, so far from my
family, has been difficult for me. The girls like it,
however, and my husband wouldn't be anywhere
else."

After Sam and Mary left early in the evening to
go to their hotel, Mary said, "Mrs. Norris is a lovely
woman, but I'm concerned about her. She seems so
fragile and ill."

"I know what you mean," Sam agreed. "Life on the mission field is not easy. I'll ask Reverend Norris if she's been to a doctor lately."

Eleven days later, Sam and Mary received the sad news that Mrs. Norris had died of typhoid fever.

Sam and Mary toured Calcutta, and saw many contrasts. Calcutta, often called the "city of palaces," was dotted with large open squares and pools of water. Houses of the wealthy were large, two story buildings made of "chunam" (brick and stucco), and surrounded by beautiful gardens. But for every palatial house, there were hundreds of small, poor dwellings, and people dressed in rags.

The Smiths rode past Fort Williams, which was bristling with soldiers and armaments. A few miles further, they saw an ornate palace where the King of Oude lived in exile. The king was allowed to wander the grounds of the palace freely, but could never leave. The British government feared that he might start a rebellion if he were given his freedom. As the Smith's carriage passed the gates, an immense cloud of pigeons soared over the palace grounds.

"The king amuses himself by keeping pigeons," the guide explained.

"See how freely they fly," Mary said, as the pigeons reeled to the right, and then the left over their heads.

Sam frowned and gazed through the grillwork on the hugh gates that were guarded day and night by British soldiers. "It's a bitter contrast," he said, "as if the king enjoys the freedom of the birds because he is imprisoned."

In a remote part of Calcutta, Sam and Mary visited a sacred shrine to the Hindu goddess Kali. Close by were other shrines for Brahma, Vishnu, Siva, and Juggernaut. The Ganges River, where sewage was dumped, ran by the shrines. In an arm of the polluted

river, Sam and Mary were surprised to see people
wading in the water, and carrying water in bowls from
the river to pour on the shrines.

"What are they doing?" Sam asked the guide.

"This is a holy place," the guide replied. "Hindu
people believe that bathing in the water here will
cleanse away their sins and heal their sicknesses. They
carry the holy water to the shrines to make peace with
their gods."

Sam watched sadly as people knelt and prayed to
the stone statues that could neither hear nor see, let
alone answer their prayers.

With intense and increasing interest, Sam visited
many of the missionary and educational institutions
in Calcutta. He was impressed with both the Christian and secular schools. He wrote to his friends in
America:

> If only the minds of the young are stimulated to
> think, if only they are aroused to question the
> truthfulness of their effete systems, and to test the
> stable foundations of Christianity, they cannot fail
> to be prepared for the overthrow of heathenism,
> which is sure to come. Delay in the work is not defeat;
> and time spent in digging, and in laying broad and
> deep foundations, is not lost. The mighty structure
> which God is rearing for his own glory is not the work
> of a day. Like the giant oak it grows slowly; but it
> is to last for an eternity.

The Smiths visited the Botanical Gardens, where
every plant growing in India could be found. Among
the curiosities were two banyon trees: one called the
Picnic Banyan, and the other the Great Banyan, the
second largest banyan tree in the world.

"See those bamboo tubes hanging from the
branches?" Sam asked, as he and Mary walked in
the shade of the Great Banyan. "New roots grow

inside those protective tubes. When the roots reach the ground, they'll form new trunks. That's how a single tree becomes a forest.''

From Calcutta, the Smiths traveled to Madras on the steamer, *Manora*. Madras was a great commercial seaport, although no ships could approach the shore. Both passenger steamers and freighters had to anchor in the bay beyond the great waves which swelled and crashed along the coast.

Sam and Mary were shocked to learn that all passengers would be carried to shore on the shoulders of coolies. ''At least it's another story to write home about,'' said Sam with a laugh.

Freight was ferried to shore in large boats that were sewn together instead of nailed, as nails could not have endured the strong surf.

''You could write about those strange little sailboats, too,'' Mary added. She and Sam watched several of the narrow outriggers skimming rapidly over the crests of the waves. Each was carved from a log barely wide enough for one kneeling person. A second log, six or eight inches in diameter was attached to the main one by two curved sticks. This provided stability in the rough water.

''Those boats aren't made for beef eaters like us,'' commented Sam. ''They're only for rice eaters.''

After spending a few days in Madras with a friend from Boston, the Smiths boarded a much larger native boat, called a ''budgerow,'' to travel nearly a hundred miles to Nellore where the first Christian mission in India was founded many years before.

When the budgerow moored at Nellore, Sam and Mary were surprised to see an American-style covered wagon waiting for them. But there was not an ox or horse in sight to pull the wagon.

Sam shrugged. ''I'm sure this must be the wagon

we are supposed to take to the mission station.''

"You must be right," Mary agreed, noticing the men who were stowing the Smith's trunks in the wagon's bed. She whispered, "They seem to know what they are doing."

The coolies soon announced that they were ready. "Let's climb up," Sam said, and he gave Mary a hand.

As soon as the Smiths were safely seated, the men who had carried their luggage divided themselves into two teams. Three of them stood in front of the wagon, and two got behind it. With a mighty groan, the men began to push and pull the wagon until it was rolling along the road. Sam and Mary glanced at each other and smiled. They both were thinking about the reports they would send home.

The coolies kept up a rapid trot during the entire fifteen-mile trip, except for the times they stopped to change places. The journey took about two hours, and at the end they seemed as fresh and lively as they had been before they began.

Telugu people with outstretched hands warmly greeted Sam and Mary when the wagon stopped.

"This is Konakiah," said Mr. Downie, the Smith's missionary host. "He is an ordained Telugu preacher and our right-hand man on the mission compound."

Konakiah stepped forward to shake hands with Sam and Mary. Sam was impressed by Konakiah's strong, wise face. Mr. Downie later told the Smiths that Konakiah could easily work for the British government for a large salary, but that he chose instead to accept less than two hundred dollars a year to do the Lord's work.

"He sees to everything around the mission," Mrs. Downie added. "He is strong enough for every emergency, willing to do any kind of work, and he loves the gospel truth."

"His name is familiar to us," Sam said. "We've read about him for years in letters from missionaries."

"It is as if we were meeting an old friend," Mary added graciously."

At Sunday worship, Sam and Mary once again heard the strange, wild Telugu music. Konakiah introduced Sam to the people as the author of the American national anthem, *Yankee Doodle*. Sam bit his lip and didn't dare glance at Mary for fear they would both laugh and embarrass the well-intentioned Konakiah.

Sam spoke about his long interest in the Telugu mission. Konakiah translated into Telugu. "I am indeed pleased to tell you the story of your mission— the Lone Star. In one dark period long ago, it was proposed that the Telugu work be closed, but Dr. Judson pleaded for you people, and we in America raised money so the mission could continue. Now I am happy to see how God's grace has made things new."

After his speech, Sam turned to Konakiah, shook his hand, and said, "This is a warm greeting from the Christians in America to the Christians among the Telugus. It was worth the journey halfway around the world to experience the joy of this hour."

Sam and Mary visited many small Telugu villages. The people were poor—of the lowest caste, or no caste at all. One man, a widower, lived alone in a small whitewashed cottage. Although it was neat and clean, the only furniture he had was a small box, a cord on which he hung his spare garments, two or three straw mats, and several water jars.

The Smiths noticed that many people in the villages were weak and shriveled. "There has been famine," their guide told them. "These people have survived, but many died."

"We see many children, but not many old people," Mary observed.

"Life is hard for Telugu people," the guide said. "They work at hard manual labor, and suffer from deadly diseases."

Sam wrote home about a little girl nine or ten years old who said to Mary and him, "I believe in Jesus, and I love Him this much." To illustrate, she opened her arms as wide as they would stretch.

After many happy weeks visiting Telugu villages, it was time for Sam and Mary to return to Madras on the first leg of their long journey home to Newton.

At Madras, Sam and Mary were guests of Dr. and Mrs. Jewett, native Bostonians. The Jewetts had founded the Telugu mission in Madras and had spent most of their lives among the Telugu people. Dr. Jewett had translated part of the Bible into Telugu.

As they toured the city, Sam and Mary saw thousands of people swarming in the streets. The wealthy lived along the beach to enjoy the clean ocean air. Their road was constantly watered to keep down the dust, and it was a fashionable drive. Elegant carriages paraded up and down.

Most people in the rest of Madras were coolies, children, artisans, and Indian and Eurasian shopkeepers. Sam and Mary were amazed at the amount of commerce in Madras.

Dr. Jewett told them, "You can buy almost anything you can think of here in Madras—except ice skates."

"Back home our grandchildren are probably skating on Crystal Lake or Bulloughs Pond today," Sam said, "and here we are fanning ourselves to keep cool."

At the mission, there was a large bowl just inside the door. Sam noticed that Indians dropped small contributions of rice into the bowl. Sometimes it was only a spoonful. A few brought their offerings tied up in the corners of sashes. When the bowl was full, the rice was sold and the money was used to support the mission.

Dr. Jewett was especially proud of the educational opportunities that the mission provided to the people. At one school where Sam and Mary visited, children hung garlands of flowers to welcome their American guests. Their excited faces were clean and radiant as they presented roses to Mary. One child brought his father to watch the ceremony. The father smiled as his child played a part in the exercises.

"Not every child is so fortunate," Dr. Jewett said, indicating a crowd of unbathed village children who had gathered to see what was going on. "It's tragic that educational opportunities sometimes cause families to be divided. Friends and even family members often ridicule those who want an education. It takes courage for many of these people to come, or send their children to school here."

Dr. Jewett introduced the Smiths to a young teacher. "My relatives threaten to kidnap me and forcibly take me away from school," she told them. "But as long as I stay on the mission grounds they can't touch me. I am afraid to leave because I might never be able to return."

The Smiths said goodbye to the Jewetts and to their new friends in Madras. They sailed on a steamship for three days across calm ocean water. Then low shores, green trees, blue hills, and mountains appeared on the horizon as the ship approached Ceylon.

When the ship docked at Point de Galle, Sam hurried down the gangplank and into the town. There he sent a telegram telling Daniel that they had arrived safely in Ceylon. Then he raced back to the ship, which sailed on to Colombo on the southwestern side of the island.

Sam and Mary rode in a carriage toward their host's home on the hillside above Colombo. Gardens and groves bordered the streets. Bright sunlight twinkled on the ocean. "This must be what the Garden of Eden was like," Mary said.

"I'm sure if we looked hard enough," Sam said, "we could even find a snake to complete it."

The next day their host, Mr. Ferguson, took the Smiths around Ceylon. Sam and Mary were impressed by the agriculture. Nearly a million acres of and were under cultivation with rice and other grains.

"We've seen rice, coffee, coconuts, and tea growing," Sam said, "but the crop in that field is new to me."

"That is cinnamon," said Mr. Ferguson.

"I never realized that cinnamon bark came from such small shrubs," Mary exclaimed.

"The shrubs could grow much larger if they were allowed to," Mr. Ferguson explained, "but planters cut the young rods as soon as the plant is large enough to produce a good profit."

Sam reached out and plucked one leaf from a cinnamon bush. He crushed it between his fingers and held it out for Mary to smell.

"That smells just like cloves," Mary said.

"Oil of cloves," Mr. Ferguson corrected. "Cinnamon is a good crop because every part of the plant is used for something. The bark is cinnamon, the leaves produce oil of cloves, and camphor comes from the roots."

Sam watched field workers stooping over cinnamon plants in the glaring heat of the day. "When we get home, we'll never take any of these things for granted again," Sam said.

Sam was fascinated by the production of plumbago, which was one of Ceylon's leading industries.

"Plumbago is excavated from mines," Mr. Ferguson told him. "Many natives are employed by the mines. The plumbago found here is very pure, and there is a lot of it."

"I know that it's imported by the United States," Sam said. "It's used for lead pencils that are manufactured in Jersey City, New Jersey. I wonder how many pencils I've used in my lifetime whose lead came from these mines?"

Sam and Mary visited mission schools. Sam was especially interested to learn that Christian work in Ceylon came about because of John Eliot's work with Indians near Newton, Massachusetts, long before the Revolutionary War. Eliot's enthusiastic letters to his friends in Europe described how he was able to teach the American natives about Jesus Christ. Dutch merchants who were trading in Ceylon read Eliot's letters and decided that it was time to bring the gospel to Ceylon. Thus the Dutch mission there was started.

Too soon, it was time for Sam and Mary to leave Ceylon. As the horizon faded into nothingness, Sam said, "We have traveled halfway around the world, my dear. We've experienced primitive jungles, seen modern cities, visited Daniel and Sarah, and have seen with our own eyes how successful missions are and how wonderful is the spirit and example of dedicated missionaries."

The second half of the Smiths' journey would take them through old cities and beautiful scenes of Europe before returning to Newton Centre.

At Home in Newton Centre

Banners and bright streamers announced a happy gathering at the Smith home. Carriages lined the street as the guests began to arrive.

"Hurry, Father," Carrie said, motioning for Sam to stand near the front door. "Where's Mother? The first guests are already here."

"She's never late," Sam said, and glanced up the staircase. "That must mean these guests are early."

"Oh, Father," Carrie said with exasperation. "I just want everything to be perfect for you today."

"No need to worry," Sam told his daughter. "You children shouldn't have gone to all the trouble. But I'm glad you did."

Mary's gown rustled as she slowly descended the stairs and stood beside Sam.

"You're as lovely today as the day I married you," Sam whispered to Mary, "—fifty years ago."

"You always say the right thing, Sam," Mary said,

and slipped her arm through his. "I guess that's because you're a poet."

"Happy anniversary!" the guests shouted as they entered the Smiths' home. "And welcome home from your trip to the other side of the world."

Sam was sorry that his good friend, Lowell Mason, was not alive to be part of the joyful occasion, but his Harvard friends, "the boys," were all there. John Greenleaf Whittier proposed a toast. "To *America*, Sam's song of our country that is sung on sea or land, in any part of the world, wherever Americans are found."

"Have I ever told you how jealous I was of you, John?" Sam confided, chuckling. "When Lowell told me that you and Mary were close friends, I was worried that I might have competition. Then Lowell assured me that you two were *just* friends." Sam gripped John's shoulder. "What a wonderful friend you have been to both Mary and me."

Oliver Holmes brought gales of laughter as he recalled college days and meetings at the Parker House restaurant. "And didn't we make a din! We had singing, too. Friend Smith gave *My Country, 'tis of Thee* and he's nearly tone deaf. You never heard anything like it. A rare old boy is Smith, I tell you. It wasn't a melancholy party!"

"As I recall, you weren't too impressed by my lyrics," Sam reminded Oliver. To everyone's delight, Sam mimicked Oliver's voice, repeating Oliver's own words, "What do you mean, Sam, when you say 'that above'?" Sam's eyes twinkled merrily. "At our ages, Oliver, we will both soon know what 'that above' means."

After all the guests had spoken, Sam stood up and asked Mary to stand beside him. "I've composed a poem for you, Mary, in honor of our fifty years together."

These fifty years of wedded love,
How brief and few they seem,
Swift as a summer day of joy,
Eventful as a dream.

Behold, dear wife, how things have changed
Through sunshine and through showers;
The spring has ripened into fall,
The buds have turned to flowers.

What long, wide paths our feet have trod
Since the far days of old!
But love has changed each woe to good,
The silver moon to gold.

When Sam had finished all nine verses, their guests applauded. Then they formed a circle, clasping hands. Their frail voices filled the room with the four verses of "My country, 'tis of thee, sweet land of liberty."

During the years that Sam and Mary lived in Newton, they saw many changes—street lights, paved roads, a police force, a water system, and fire alarms. Automobiles occasionally rumbled along Center Street. Sam absolutely refused to ride in one. He much preferred the safety of his horse and buggy.

In 1888, Newton celebrated its two hundredth anniversary as a city, Sam was invited to take part in that celebration. At a banquet at the Woodland Park Hotel, one hundred specially invited guests heard him read:

> With filial love and reverent thoughts we scan
> The glimmering dawn in which the town began;
> When, one by one, with spirits brave and true,
> The founders left the old, and sought the new;
> Pitched their frail tents upon the virgin sod,
> Indians their neighbors, and their helper, God;
> Taught the wild savage from rude strife to cease,
> And learn the nobler arts of love and peace.

The evening concluded with the singing of *America.*

As Sam and Mary grew older, they preferred to spend winters in rented quarters in Boston. Friends dropped in nearly every day to visit, and the Smiths received letters from friends all over the world.

Sam's and Mary's sixtieth wedding anniversary, in September, 1894, was a quiet affair. Only their children, grandchildren, and close friends attended. After the party, Mary commented, "I don't think Oliver looks well. He didn't seem to have his usual spark of humor."

One of the saddest days of Sam's life was when Oliver Holmes died. "Life will never be the same without his laughter," Sam told Mary. "His playful reference to my being 'disguised under the universal name of Smith' never hurt my sensibilities, but was one of the merry things we enjoyed together." In tribute, Sam wrote:

> Dear master of the tuneful lyre,
> How shall we breathe the word Farewell?
> How shall we touch the trembling wire
> Which vibrates with thy mystic spell?
>
> The world seems poor, of thee bereft,
> The evening sky without the sun,
> The setting, not the gem, is left;
> The frame remains, the picture gone.

When Sam was eighty-seven, an editorial in the *Boston Post* suggested that:

> Too often we wait until someone great has died before we priaise him. Now is the time to reward him [Smith]. Nothing has done so much to unite this country as the national hymn, *America*.

Everyone agreed enthusiastically, and plans for "the celebration of the century" began to take shape. It was to be the biggest event ever in the city of Boston. An afternoon session was planned for children and out-of-town guests. Two hundred Eliot School children would sing *America*. An evening session would be for local people. The United States Marine Band would play patriotic music. Both the Harvard Glee Club and the Handel & Haydn Society would sing. Governor Greenhalge would present Sam to the audience.

The entire country caught the spirit. The Columbian Bell in Washington, D. C., was to ring at exactly noon. All across the nation, school children would sing *America*. It would, indeed, be "the celebration of the century," to honor a man who was alive.

Sam wrote to one of his sons,

> We shall be very happy to welcome you, April 3, if you are able to come; though the gratification of two or three hours, it would seem, could hardly pay you for so long a journey. Still, it is a thing that occurs

only once in a lifetime—like the smallpox—and I do not wonder that it has attraction for you.

Boston bustled with activities leading up to the celebration. Every day the newspapers carried accounts of bell ringings and speeches and school programs. The Smith home was filled with flowers, and messages from all over the world constantly poured in. Governors from every state sent congratulatory messages.

Mary could hardly find time to carry on her household chores, but late one evening she wrote a letter to one of her daughters expressing concern for Sam.

> I shall be so relieved when it is over, I think it has worn upon your father, but he will not confess it. He cannot help feeling grateful. Just now, more telegrams have come, and magnificent flowers.

The huge celebration progressed exactly as planned. Overflowing crowds jammed the Music Hall, which was decorated with red, white, and blue banners. Sam proudly wore a bunch of violets that had been sent "with love and respect" from children in Seattle, Washington. He was thrilled when the Eliot School students sang his words, reminding him of the first time he had heard them at the Park Street Church steps. How he wished Lowell Mason could have been there!

In the evening, Sam was escorted to the Music Hall by a military band and soldier guard of honor. Deafening shouts and applause rang out as Governor Greenhalge introduced Sam to the audience. Sam stood at the podium and felt overwhelmed by the crowd's affection. When the cheers died down, Sam began speaking in his now frail voice:

A friend, Mr. Lowell Mason, gave me a quantity of music books in the German language, for translating. On a dismal day in February, about half an hour before sunset, I was turning over the leaves of one of the music books, when my eye rested on the tune which is now known as *America*. I liked the spirited movement of it, not knowing at that time it was *God Save the King*. I glanced at the German words and saw that they were patriotic, and instantly felt an impulse to write a patriotic hymn of my own, adapted to the tune. Picking up a scrap of waste paper, which lay near me, I wrote, probably within a half hour, the hymn *America*, as it is now known everywhere. The hymn stands today as it stood on the bit of waste paper, five or six inches long and two and a half inches wide.

To my surprise, I found later that Mr. Mason had incorporated it into a program for the celebration of July 4, 1831, at the Park Street Church in Boston. I have since heard it sung in many languages, more than halfway round the world, the latest translation being in Hebrew.

When it was composed, I was profoundly impressed with the necessary relation between love of God and love of Country, and I rejoice if the expression of my own sentiments and convictions still find an answering chord in the hearts of my countrymen.

I pray that the spirit of these simple verses may be the spirit of people forever.

Before Sam could return to his seat, Mary was called to the platform. A gift of two thousand dollars was presented to them. The closing of the "celebration of the century" was the thrilling sound of hundreds of people singing, "My country, 'tis of thee, sweet land of liberty, of thee I sing . . ."

Late that evening, when Samuel and Mary sat in the parlor, surrounded by mementos of the celebration, Samuel shook his head sadly. In a quiet voice he said, "I regret that my dear friends, Oliver and Lowell, did not live to see this day."

The famous artist, George Piexotto, was engaged to paint Sam's portrait. It took a bit of coaxing to get him to sit still long enough for the artist to capture his image. In May, 1895, the portrait was hung in the Harvard College Library.

One day in the early summer of 1895, Samuel's daughter Mary asked him to walk with her through the old North End. As they sauntered along narrow streets and passed familiar places, Samuel recalled events and people of long before.

At eighty-seven Sam still stood straight and tall. His hearing was not as keen as it was when he was young, and his voice was not as strong. However, he was still a handsome gentleman. He and Mary walked slowly, glancing into shop windows and looking at buildings.

"I remember the Sunday afternoon my parents took me for a walk," he reminisced. "It was the fortieth anniversary of Paul Revere's ride, and old Mr. Revere was still alive. Even though I was a child, I remember this."

At 37 Sheafe Street, Sam said, "This is where I was born. The house has been torn down and re-placed, though. I wish I could recall my first poem, *Elegy on a Cat*. I was eight years old, and was in Eliot School. The verses have completely left my mind." Chuckling, he added, "I'm certain the cat, too is gone."

At the old apothecary shop, Samuel stopped. "Here I took my first step. Mother asked if I could go it alone, and I said I could. I recall looking straight at the figure of Hippocrates on top of that red post." He laughed again. "Like the cat, Hippocrates has vanished, but the red post is still here."

A sea breeze blowing over the harbor refreshed Sam and Mary as they approached Lewis Wharf. The old sign over his father's barrel shop had been torn down long ago. The place was now used for storage.

"I spent many hours on the wharf putting bands on barrels." Sam's voice trembled a little. "Not as many as I wish I had. Perhaps Father wouldn't have died so young if I could have helped him more."

"Now I'd like to walk by Old North Church," Sam said.

By the time they reached Christ Church, known as Old North Church, Sam was ready to rest. Sitting on the steps, just as he had done many years before, he recalled in great detail how Sexton Perry had shown him the lanterns and taken him into the crypt. "I was so frightened I thought my heart would pound right through my shirt." Sam chuckled. "The shirt was torn on a nail and was very dirty. Mother noticed the condition of my shirt, but I didn't tell my parents about my excursion until I was grown up. I don't know why I didn't tell them then, unless it was fear of scolding or punishment. Perhaps it was the fact that I had a secret. A few years ago I told your mother. I must have felt that I was finally clearing my conscience."

"I'm glad you told me the story now, Father." Mary was chuckling too.

Before leaving the church, Sam gazed for a moment at the belfry tower. "I count it to have been a happy lot, and possibly the inspiration to my choice of profession, that I was born under the sound of the Old North Church chimes," he told Mary.

"Let's go to Copp's Hill next," suggested Sam. "I want to see again the bullet holes in Captain Malcolm's gravestone."

Walking up the incline of the hill to the burying

ground, Sam began to recite the words he had learned as a boy: "Here lies buried in a stone grave ten feet deep—"

"—Captain Daniel Malcolm," Mary injected dramatically."

"—Merchant," Sam joined in again. They completed the recitation in u..ison and then laughed merrily.

From the burying ground, they walked to Faneuil Hall. Gazing up at the weathervane, Sam asked his daughter, "Do you know that the grasshopper is hollow? Just five years ago it was refurbished and I know from a reliable source that the man who did the repair placed a copper cylinder inside it. On it is engraved, 'Lunch for the grasshopper from the City, March 26, 1889,' Inside the cylinder are copies of Boston newspapers of that date and an annual city report."

"I wonder how long the grasshopper will keep his secret," Mary said. Neither Sam nor Mary could know that fifty years later the grashopper would be taken down again, and the "lunch" discovered. They also couldn't know that eighty years in the future the grasshopper would be stolen—by helicopter—but found, repaired, and replaced on its historical perch.

Near the end of their walk, Sam and Mary stood in front of Park Street Church. Overcome with emotion, Sam's eyes welled with tears. "I was shocked when I heard my simple verses sung here. That was the day I met your mother. Little did I realize then that she and I would spend sixty-one years together. She has been the greatest blessing of my life."

"I think you've walked enough for one day, Father," Mary said. "You must be tired. But I'm glad we took this walk together. It will be one of my cherished memories." She kissed her father's wrinkled cheek.

"I'm ready to go home," Sam admitted. "I need to do some studying."

"Studying!" Mary exclaimed. "What in the world are you learning now?"

"Russian," Sam replied, "so I can read the Bible in that language. It is delightful to tackle a new language. I just love it."

In July, 1895, Sam was invited to take part in a Christian Endeavor Convention, where eleven thousand young people met under a huge tent on Boston Common. When Sam stepped forward to read the poem he had composed for the occasion, there was thunderous applause. The program ended, of course, with the singing of *America*. Afterward, people encircled Sam and begged him to write and autograph his verses. One woman remarked, "Oh, Dr. Smith, I do hope my mansion in Heaven will be right beside yours, so I can hear you talk all the time."

On Saturday, November 16, 1895, Sam joined the remainder of "the boys" for luncheon at the Parker House. When he left the restaurant, he glanced at his pocket watch. He had just enough time to catch the train at South Station, for Readville, where he was scheduled to preach on Sunday.

Before the train left the station, a friend passed through the car and spoke to Sam. When he didn't reply, the man ran to get help.

Sam was carried from the train to the station waiting room. An ambulance and doctor arrived in less than ten minutes, but it was too late.

Sam's grandson, who worked at the South Station, heard the ambulance siren, but did not know that his grandfather had died until he read the evening newspaper.

In a sermon that Sam had preached a short time before, at the Newton Centre Church, he said:

So let our lives pass sweetly onward from Sabbath
to Sabbath, and from year to year, until suddenly,
at some appointed time, we shall be permitted to
change the earthly for the heavenly temple; the music
of earth fading from our ears, only to be exchanged
for the music of Heaven, whose sweetness shall never
end.

As a final farewell to Sam, *America* was sung at his
funeral in his beloved church. His grave is in Newton
Cemetery, near many of those he loved and served
for so many years.

America Remembers Samuel Francis Smith

The words that Samuel Smith penned on a scrap of paper more than a century ago continue to evoke strong sentiments toward God and Country whenever the song is sung. *America* has been embraced as the national hymn of the United States of America. Friends of patriotism assure a future for this song and remembrance for its writer.

Most encyclopedias state that the song was composed in 1832. The error is understandable, because although Mr. Smith's verses were first sung on the Park Street Church steps in 1831, there was no title or author named on the program that day. The first time the verses were printed with music, title, and author's name was in 1832 in a music journal, *The Choir*, edited by Lowell Mason. All five verses were printed.

Lowell Mason was an educator as well as a composer. He introduced music education in the public schools of Boston through a book of songs he compiled. The book was titled *The Juvenile Lyre*, and included *America* under the 1832 date.

After the song received international recognition, Samuel Smith became a world celebrity. He was often asked to write and autograph his famous verses. As Smith grew older and forgot the exact details, he used the year 1832 because it had become the accepted date. One such autographed copy of *America* is preserved in the Boston Public Library. Mr. Smith's descendants also have handwritten copies. Over the years the error of the date has been compounded.

Memorials have been dedicated to Samuel Francis Smith and his achievements. Two years after his death, a tablet was placed on the site of his birthplace on Sheafe Street. It reads:

Birthplace of
Rev. S. F. Smith, D.D.
Author of *America*
1808 - 1895
Erected by the
Old South Chapter
Daughters of the American Revolution
1897

In 1898, a chime of bells was installed in the First Baptist Church tower in Newton as a memorial to Smith.

In October, 1908, the City of Newton celebrated what would have been Samuel Smith's one hundredth birthday. That same year, Mrs. Hitchings' house in Andover was designated the *America House*.

While reviewing his father's mementos, Daniel Smith discovered the original scrap of paper containing the verses. It clearly showed the cut where the middle verse had been removed. In 1914, Daniel presented the paper to Harvard College Library.

Newspaper items about the gift continued to claim the composing year as 1832.

Copies of the program printed for the 1831 Independence Day celebration at the Park Street Church were given to the Chapin Library, Williams College, Williamstown, Massachusetts; the library of the American Antiquarian Society, in Worchester, Massachusetts; and to Mr. Henry Lowell Mason, grandson of Lowell Mason. No one noticed the discrepancy in the date.

In 1919, on the one hundred eleventh anniversary of Smith's birth, the Newton Centre Woman's Club placed a stone at the edge of the sidewalk in front of the Smith home. It, too, bears the 1832 date. Smith's granddaughter, Miss Annie Smith, unveiled the tablet, and *America* was sung by the Rice School children.

Others in Smith's family unwittingly carried on the error. In 1932, his grandson, the Honorable Nelson Glazier Morton, wrote an article for a Boston newspaper that told how his grandfather wrote the verses in 1832.

The First Baptist Church in Newton voted to dedicate the memorial chimes to Smith. On February 28, 1932 the congregation sang hymns composed by Samuel Smith, and then read the following dedication in unison:

> We are dedicating the Tower of the Church today as the 'America Tower,' in commemoration of the one hundredth anniversary of the writing of the hymn *America*, by Reverend Samuel Francis Smith, D.D., in February, 1832. Dr. Smith was once Pastor of this church for twelve years, and the chimes in the Tower are a memorial to him. The inscription which is unveiled today reads as follows:

1932
"America"
Tower
in honor of
Samuel F. Smith
Author 1832
Pastor 1842 - 1854

On Sundays, holidays, and voting days, the bells in the "American Tower" ring out, "My country, 'tis of thee, sweet land of liberty. . . ."

Even though Smith lived in Newton, he remained a trustee of the Waterville College (now Colby College) for twenty years, In honor of the one hundredth anniversary of his song, a tablet was unveiled on the campus, also bearing the 1832 date.

The United states Congress carried on the error. On June 16, 1932, it passed a resolution "that appropriate observances be held throughout the nation, in commemoration of the writing of our national hymn."

In 1935, an article appearing in a Boston newspaper tried to straighten out the error. In included a picture of the July 4, 1831, program and quotes from several 1831 newspaper accounts of the Park Street Church celebration. But the error persists today.

Smith descendants continued to live in the house on Center Street until 1954, when the property was left vacant. Soon it became shabby and needed repairs. In 1958, a sign posted in the front yard announced that the Smith homestead would be sold at auction. Fifty concerned Newton residents immediately formed the Samuel Francis Smith Homestead Society, Incorporated. They aimed to restore the property as a national landmark. No federal funds could be used, however, since Samuel Smith had not been born in the house. It was up to the people of Newton to supply the money and manpower to restore the old house.

The Homestead Society circulated a leaflet that told Newton residents, "If It Goes, It's Gone Forever." On Samuel Smith's one hundred fiftieth birthday anniversary, seventeen thousand Newton school children participated in a drive to raise money. Special assemblies and programs were held in their schools, and children raised more than one thousand dollars.

Boy Scouts and Campfire Girls cleaned the grounds, and promised to maintain them after the property was purchased. Campfire Girls provided two flags to fly over the homestead—the contemporary American flag, and "Old Glory," the flag of 1831.

Because members of the Smith family had always lived in the house, the Homestead Society found much material that belonged to Sam and Mary when the house was renovated. The Society also recovered some of the Smith's original furniture to place in the house. Other individuals donated furnishings that were commonly found in houses during Sam and Mary Smith's lifetimes.

It took eleven years to restore the Smith home to some likeness of its original condition. Then it served as a museum for Smith memorabilia, including copies of most of Samuel Smith's books and diaries, irreplaceable material.

On the night of July 5, 1969, fire engines raced to 1181 Center Street. But it was too late. When the blazing fire was extinguished, Samuel Smith's home was nothing more than a charred wreckage in a cellar hole. The words of the leaflet, "If It's Gone, It's Gone Forever," had come true.

The bronze plaque on the granite stone placed there in 1897 still stands. A tulip tree grows where the house once stood. The grass is neatly mowed and the shrubs are trimmed. The well-kept vacant lot, in the heart of busy Newton Centre, is a silent memorial to a beloved and patriotic man.

Tourists visiting in Boston often go to the "Old North Church of Paul Revere Fame." Each year on April 18, Paul Revere's ride is re-enacted following an early evening worship service in the sanctuary. A descendant of either Paul Revere, Robert Newman, or William Dawes (chosen alternately) has the honor of carrying two lighted lanterns to the belfry steeple. Samuel Smith would have enjoyed the traditional singing of *America* during the ceremony each year.

Oliver Wendell Homes once wrote, "When all the poets are gone and forgotten, there will live the name of the man who wrote 'My Country, 'tis of thee.' And the reason is very plain to see. He said, '*My* Country!' That '*My*' made it a national anthem."

Although the *Star Spangled Banner* was officially designated by Congress as America's "national anthem," it has not replaced *America* in the hearts of American citizens. It is probably sung more than any other patriotic song, and the people have adopted it as our "national hymn."

The finest tribute to Samuel Francis Smith is the patriotic feeling that his famous words continue to stir in millions of Americans around the world. Sung by children and adults of all races and creeds, at all kinds of public and private gatherings, both religious and secular, *America* is our perpetual heritage.

BIBLIOGRAPHY

A Guide at a Glance of Historic Boston (Winchester MA: Rawding Distributing Company, 1974).

Alvord, Douglas, *An Illustrated History and Guide to the Faneuil Hall Marketplace* (Boston: Alice Atwood Productions, 1978).

Andrews, Charles M., *Our Earliest Colonial Settlements* (Ithaca NY: Cornell University Press, 1959).

Booth, John Nichols, *The Story of the Second Church* (1958).

Bowen, Catherine Drinker, *Yankee from Olympus* (Boston: Little, Brown & Co., 1944).

Clark, David L., *Christ Church, The Old North Church* (Medford MA: First National Bank of Boston, with Massachusetts Dept. of Commerce and Development, Acme Printing Co.).

Clark, David L., *The Old North Church in Picture and in Story* (Medford MA: Acme Printing Co.).

Crosby, H. Englizian, *Brimstone Corner: Park Street Church, Boston* (Chicago: Moody Press, 1968).

Crowell, Thomas Y., *Under the Old Elms* (1895).

Earle, Alice Morse, *Customs and Fashions in Old New England* (Rutland VT: Charles E. Tuttle Co., 1894; reprint 1973).

Earle, Alice Morse, *Home Life in Colonial Days* (Stockbridge MA: Berkshire Traveller Press, 1898. Reprint New York: Grosset & Dunlap, 1974).

Earle, Alice Morse, *Two Centuries of Costume in America* (2 vol.; New York: MacMillan Co., 1903. Reprint Williamstown MA: Corner House Publishers, 1974).

Fitts, Ralph Corydon, *Research* (Newton Centre MA: Smith Homestead, about 1950).

Lord, Walter, *The Dawn's Early Light* (New York: Norton & Co. Reprint New York: Dell Publishing Co., 1972).

Marsen, Philip, *Boston Latin School, Breeder of Democracy* (Cambridge MA: University Press, 1963).

Marshall family, *Marshall Family History*.

Marshall, Jane, *America: Hymn of the Noble Free* (Unpublished thesis, 1968).

Marshall, John F., *Tales and Traditions of the Family of Harry and Emma Marshall* (Newton Centre MA: Smith Homestead, 1967).

Morton, W. F. (daughter of S. F. Smith), *Memories of the Author of 'America'* (Newton Centre MA: Smith Homestead, early 1900s).

Rowe, Henry K., *Tercentenary History of Newton* (Newton MA: Property of Newton Public Library).

Sawtelle, Clement C., *The Nineteenth of April, 1775, A Collection of First Hand Accounts* (Lincoln MA: Sawtelle of Somerset, 1968).

Sheets, Robert Newman, *Robert Newman* (Denver: Newman Family Society, Colombia Press, 1975).

Smith, Samuel Francis, *Rambles in Mission Fields* (Boston: W. G. Corthell, Mission Rooms, 1883).

Van Doren, Carl, *Secret History of the American Revolution* (New York: Popular Library, 1941).

Weeks, Edward, *Boston, Cradle of Liberty* (New York: Arts, Inc., 1941).

Welcome to the Freedom Trail and the Many Worlds of Boston (Boston: Freedom Trail Foundation, Inc.; distributed by John Hancock Life Insurance Company).

Wertenbaker, Thomas J., *The Golden Age of Colonial Culture* (Ithaca NY: Cornell University Press, 1949).

INDEX

ABOUT THE AUTHOR

Marguerite Fitch worked for many years as a school secretary in Newton Centre, Massachusetts, the town where Samuel Francis Smith had lived one hundred years earlier. Two things happened there which started her on the way to this book. First, school children contributed money to save the old Smith Homestead from an auctioneer's block. Second, she noticed that her school library had no books about Smith.

While still in Newton Centre, she studied primary source materials and contacted Smith descendents living in the area. Later, she moved to California and began work on this book and other writings. She also speaks in public schools, helping to make history come alive for children. The city of Lakewood presented her with an award for outstanding service to school children. Mrs. Fitch now lives in Seal Beach, California, with her husband Edson.

ABOUT THE ARTIST

Edward Ostendorf, known as Ned. O., says, "I started drawing before I could write my name. I had a big brother who was an artist, and I thought that was the neatest thing on earth. I grew up knowing I would be an artist and attended every art class after school and on Saturday that I could find." Since then he has gone on to illustrate everything from newspapers to books.

SOWERS SERIES

Abigail Adams by Evelyn Witter

Johnny Appleseed by David Collins

George Washington Carver by David Collins

Christopher Columbus by Bennie Rhodes

George Frideric Handel by Charles Ludwig

Mahalia Jackson by Evelyn Witter

Johannes Kepler by John Hudson Tiner

Francis Scott Key by David Collins

Robert E. Lee by Lee Roddy

Abraham Lincoln by David Collins

Samuel F. B. Morse by John Hudson Tiner

Isaac Newton by John Hudson Tiner

Florence Nightingale by David Collins

Samuel Francis Smith by Marguerite Fitch

Billy Sunday by Robert Allen

Teresa of Calcutta by Jeanene Watson

George Washington by Norma Cournow Camp

Susanna Wesley by Charles Ludwig

The Wright Brothers by Charles Ludwig